POWER
OF
SPEAKING
POSITIVE

JOY HANEY

POWER OF SPEAKING POSITIVE

WORD AFLAME PRESS

Power of Speaking Positive

by Joy Haney

©2004 Joy Haney
Reprint 2006

Cover Design by Shane Long

All Scripture quotations in this book are from the King James Version of the Bible unless otherwise identified.

All rights reserved. No portion of this publication may be reproduced, stored in an electronic system, or transmitted in any form or by any means, electronic, mechanical, photocopy, recording, or otherwise, without the prior permission of Joy Haney. Brief quotations may be used in literary reviews.

Printed in United States of America

Printed by

WORD AFLAME PRESS
8855 Dunn Road, Hazelwood, MO 63042
www.pentecostalpublishing.com

Library of Congress Cataloging-in-Publication Data

Haney, Joy, 1942–
    Power of speaking positive / Joy Haney.
        p. cm.
    ISBN 1-56722-655-8 (pbk.)
1. Interpersonal communication—Religiou aspects—Christianity. 2. Oral communication—Religious aspects—Christianity. I. Title.
    BV4597.53.C64H36 2004
    248.4—dc22

2004013479

Acknowledgements

I give special thanks to the following people:

Kenneth Haney, my wonderful husband, who is a constant strength in my life.

Margie McNall, a great proofreader and author's friend.

Shane Long, for his excellent cover work.

Aleta Bird, for all her hard work.

Bethany Sledge for her efficient proofreading.

John & Marilyn McDonald, my favorite brother and his wife, for writing the foreword of this book.

To the Lord Jesus Christ, for without Him I could not write. He is my inspiration, and the anointing comes from Him.

Contents

Foreword		9
Preface		13
1.	What You Say Is What You Get!	17
2.	Speech: Language of the Soul	39
3.	The Power of Words	55
4.	The Mind Affects Speech	67
5.	Enemies of Speaking Positive	75
6.	Train Yourself to Speak Positive	89
7.	Speak Victory	109
8.	Speak Like a Winner	121
9.	Speak a Blessing	135
Epilogue		153

Foreword

There is a constant battle in the mind. Victories are won or lost by the power of the mind. This book, written by Joy Haney, will teach its readers to win the battles of life, first by how to THINK, and then by how to SPEAK!

Joy Haney not only writes in a positive manner, she lives a positive life. As she is one of my six sisters, I've known her all my life. Therefore, I can testify that she is a living example of a life that is blessed by God because of her positive approach to life. Her very presence energizes your life because of her faith. You, too, can have that same blessing and positive approach in your life as outlined in this book.

Many years ago, in my early ministry, I was visiting an elderly lady in the hospital who was suffering from a stroke. During the course of our menial conversation, I commented to her about her milk glass being half-empty. This little, feisty woman perked up and retorted, "Son, this glass is not half empty; it is half full! It's all in how you view it." We chuckled together, yet the incidental words in a nonchalant conversation gave me a revelation to life! A new way to view life! A new way to think! A new way to speak!

Leaving the hospital, those few words resounded over and over in my mind. Strangely, there was nothing profound about them, but those words absolutely changed my life from that day on. That little stranger changed my negative approach to a positive one—a lesson that has lived with me since the moment she spoke that powerful truth. The encounter that day with a few witty words was a defining moment in my life!

As I read this new book by Joy Haney that incident came to my mind. That same truth spoken by a little lady many years ago is the powerful theme of this book. Contained in the pages of this book is an opportunity for the reader to grasp a revelation of life. A revelation that Jesus taught: a revelation that is woven throughout the Word of God. It is a revelation that will unlock the prison of a negative mind to the freedom of a positive mind to become a "new creature in Christ Jesus." "Old things" and old approaches "must pass away." Jesus came to give us a more abundant life, which becomes available when the words of this book are learned and then applied. In order for that abundant life to take effect in our lives, we must be "doers of the Word," as well as "hearers of the Word."

This God-anointed book will change a negative approach to life to a positive approach to the realm where possibilities and miracles abound. A positive approach will put a smile on your lips, a spring in your steps, and a song in your heart.

This book is filled with a powerful, positive approach to direct the mind and the mouth of mankind. It will give you direction on how to change your cynicism to sweetness, your sorrow to joy, and your night to day. You will change your fear to faith, your hate to love, your depression to happiness, your shame to forgiveness, your harshness to gentleness, your badness to goodness, your stubbornness to meekness, and your excessiveness to temperance. Your judgmental spirit will change to a long-suffering spirit, and your troubled spirit will become a

Foreword

peaceful spirit. This is the more abundant life! This is heaven's approach to life.

Your life will be richer, fuller, and happier as you apply the principles of this book. The scriptures used in this book are inspiring and refreshing. Are you tired of hearing the negative reports of the news media and of those around you who constantly give an evil report? Then this book is a must-read for you! Just as anti-bacterial soap cleanses the hands, this book will cleanse your mind and your speech. It will result in mental and verbal health for yourself and then flow from you to those around you.

Truly, there is life or death in the usage of the tongue. We heal people or kill people; we bless people or curse people all with the power and usage of our tongue. Let's be challenged to not hurt with our tongue but to edify one another with our tongue.

As a minister of the gospel for forty years, I would well advise my congregation to read the Bible first, and secondly read this book. Why? Because it will enlighten whoever reads it to fulfill the will of God in their life, and to live that more *abundant life* spoken about by Jesus. For only He can change your life and make you whole by following the precepts of His Word, written about so positively in this book.

Rev. & Mrs. John R. McDonald
Senior Pastor/Full Gospel Tabernacle
Eureka, California

Preface

This book upholds and embraces the phrase in Ecclesiastes 3:7: "A time to *speak*."

As we begin our lives as helpless infants, our parents urge us to say our first word. They hold up an object, point to it, say the name that identifies it, and encourage us to repeat it.

Oh, the joy of a first word. To learn a word becomes a challenge, and then one day the baby is talking. Then the baby becomes a toddler and he or she learns to read words put together in sentences. The words in the books are often accompanied with pictures to make the meaning more clear.

Then the day comes when the child is reading pages with words on them and no pictures. They have come to a higher level of understanding. One book leads to another book, and words read become part of their understanding and knowledge.

This book is about speech, words, feelings, communication, and what binds people together. There are two classes of people identified in this book: the positive and the negative. The positive speaking people are winners; they please God and bless others. Their tongue is not as the stinger of a wasp, but it is a well of blessing.

The positive speakers are people who accomplish things in a magnificent fashion, hurting no one in the process. They draw people into their world instead of shutting them out. They are the ones who inspire and make the world a better place. Faith is their scepter, and love sits on the thrones of their hearts.

"Speak and Receive"

Seek and you shall find.
Ask and it shall be thine.
Speak to a mountain; it shall leave.
You must speak what you believe.

What you say is what you get.
Life is just what you make of it.
Give and it shall be given; you shall learn
Words that are spoken will have a return.

Bread cast upon the water will come back,
For in God's economy there is no lack.
What is spoken that will be,
For words last through an eternity.

—Joy L. Haney

1

What You Say Is What You Get!

The power of a spoken word is utterly phenomenal! Words start wars, words spoken with intensity can cause someone to kill, words spoken with forgiveness heal, words help build bridges between people or erect walls, words are the most effective tools owned by men and women.

Words are like prairie fires. Once started, they are difficult to stop. Words have the power to touch the mind, heart, spirit and soul of a person. They can be as icicles, or warm as apple pie. Words can be like razors, sharp and dangerous, or they can be soft as the fur of a kitten.

If words are so powerful, why is it that more people do not give additional attention to them—not only to the words that are said, but also to the spirit in which they are spoken? One word can be spoken many different ways and have a different meaning by *how* it is spoken. The word "hello" can be spoken curtly or friendly, in a sarcastic manner or a hateful way. It can be spoken timidly or boldly. It can be spoken any way a person feels.

There was a day when two men felt positive faith in their God and spoke it. "And Caleb stilled the people before Moses, and said, Let us go up at once, and possess it; for we are well able to overcome it" (Numbers 13:30).

"We are well able to overcome it!" Words spoken that day did not die in the ears of the Lord. God remembered what Caleb had spoken and He had a few words to say about him later: "But my servant Caleb, because he had another spirit with him, and hath followed me fully, him will I bring into the land whereinto he went; and his seed shall possess it" (Numbers 14:24).

Caleb spoke words, God heard them, and He rewarded them. All of Caleb's friends died in the wilderness, except, of course, Joshua, but the two men who spoke faith lived on for many years.

Listen to Caleb forty years later. He was still speaking like a winner: "As yet I am as strong this day as I was in the day that Moses sent me: as my strength was then, even so is my strength now, for war, both to go out, and to come in. Now therefore give me this mountain, whereof the LORD spake in that day; for thou heardest in that day how the Anakims were there, and that the cities were great and fenced: if so be the LORD will be with me, then I shall be able to drive them out, as the LORD said" (Joshua 14:11-12).

What Caleb asked of Joshua—he received just as he had spoken! Spoken words affect our future, our families, our happiness, and even our health.

Dr. Cho relates a powerful story of the effect of speech on the body in his book, *The Fourth Dimension.* One morning as he was eating breakfast with one of Korea's leading neurosurgeons, who was telling him about various medical findings on the operation of the brain, the doctor said these words: "Dr. Cho, did you know that the speech center in the brain rules over all the nerves? According to our recent findings in neurology, the speech center in the brain has total dominion over all the other nerves." He said that the speech nerve center had such power over all of the body that simply speaking can give one control over his body, to manipulate it in the way he wishes. He said, "If someone keeps on saying, 'I'm going to become weak,' then right away, all the nerves receive that message, and they say, 'Oh, let's prepare to become weak, for we've received instructions from our central communication that we should become weak.' They then in natural sequence adjust their physical attitudes to weakness."[1]

The opposite must be true when positive words of faith are spoken. After prayer is made over a health condition and the Word is read, then the mouth should start confessing with conviction these words: "I am healed according to I Peter 2:24. Strength is coming into my body. I am fearfully and wonderfully made. God is healing me; every organ in my body is receiving healing power. I am healed in Jesus' name!"

Speak it in the morning, in the noontime, throughout the day, in the evening and at night. Speak only positive faith in the face of negative facts and doubt, for in the Scriptures we are instructed to speak!

In the Beginning

The principle of the spoken word began at Creation. Genesis 1:1 states, "In the beginning God created the heaven and the earth." The third verse indicates how He did it. The earth was without form, or void, and God *spoke* the world into existence. He spoke, "Let there be," and there was. As He spoke, "Let there be fowls in the air," a bird began to fly. The power of the spoken word was demonstrated in great fashion.

> *By the word of the LORD were the heavens made; and all the host of them by the breath of his mouth. For he spake, and it was done; he commanded, and it stood fast.*
> —PSALM 33:6, 9

And God *said*, Let there be light: and there was light.

And God *said*, Let there be a firmament in the midst of the waters, and let it divide the waters from the waters. . . . and it was so.

And God *said*, Let the waters under the heaven be gathered together unto one place, and let the dry land appear: and it was so.

And God *said*, Let the earth bring forth grass, the herb yielding seed, and the fruit tree yielding fruit after his kind, whose seed is in itself, upon the earth: and it was so.

And God *said*, Let there be lights in the firmament of the heaven to divide the day from the night; and let them be for signs, and for seasons, and for days, and years: and let them be for lights in the firmament of the heaven to give light upon the earth: and it was so.

WHAT YOU SAY IS WHAT YOU GET

And God *said*, Let the waters bring forth abundantly the moving creature that hath life, and fowl that may fly above the earth in the open firmament of heaven. And God created great whales, and every living creature that moveth, which the waters brought forth abundantly, after their kind, and every winged fowl after his kind: and God saw that it was good.

And God *said*, Let the earth bring forth the living creature after his kind, cattle, and creeping thing, and beast of the earth after his kind: and it was so.

And God *said*, Let us make man in our image, after our likeness: and let them have dominion over the fish of the sea, and over the fowl of the air, and over the cattle, and over all the earth, and over every creeping thing that creepeth upon the earth. So God created man in his own image, in the image of God created he him; male and female created he them.

THE SCENARIO OF CREATION TAKEN FROM GENESIS 1:1-27

Notice God not only created the world by the spoken word, but He also spoke to that which He created:

And God blessed them, saying, Be fruitful, and multiply, and fill the waters in the seas, and let fowl multiply in the earth.

And God blessed them, and God said unto them, Be fruitful, and multiply, and replenish the earth, and subdue it: and have dominion over the fish of the sea, and over the fowl of the air, and over every living thing that moveth upon the earth. And God said, Behold, I have given you every herb bearing seed, which is upon the face of all the earth, and every tree, in the which is the fruit of a tree yielding seed; to you it shall be for meat. And to every beast of the earth, and to every fowl of the air, and to every thing that creepeth upon the earth, wherein there is life, I have given every green herb for meat: and it was so.

—GENESIS 1:22, 28-30

SPEECH IS COMMUNICATION

Speaking not only creates things, but it also communicates ideas and thoughts. After God created man, He communicated with him in strong language not to eat of the forbidden fruit. "And the LORD God commanded the man, *saying*, Of every tree of the garden thou mayest freely eat: but of the tree of the knowledge of good and evil, thou shalt not eat of it: for in the day that thou eatest thereof thou shalt surely die" (Genesis 2:16-17).

Even though Adam and Eve did eat of the forbidden fruit, and death entered into their body, the principle of speaking did not die. There is power in the spoken word.

Jesus substantiated this principle in Mark 11:22-23: "And Jesus answering saith unto them, Have faith in God. For verily I say unto you, That whosoever shall say unto this mountain, Be thou removed, and be thou cast into the sea; and shall not doubt in his heart, but shall believe that those things which he saith shall come to pass; he shall have whatsoever he saith."

What prompted Jesus to say this? It began when Jesus and His disciples had left Bethany, and Jesus was hungry. He saw a fig tree in the distance, but when He arrived to pick some figs off the tree, there were no figs, only leaves. "And Jesus answered and said unto it, No man eat fruit of thee hereafter for ever. And his disciples heard it" (Mark 11:14).

Notice the phrase, "And Jesus answered and said unto it." My question is, "What was the tree saying to Jesus?" It was speaking something, because Jesus answered it. Jesus addressed the tree. He spoke to the tree and called it a *thee*.

Jesus and His disciples were on their way to Jerusalem. When they arrived at the city, they went to the Temple, where there was much selling and merchandising. This angered Jesus and He overthrew the tables of the moneychangers and the seats of those that sold doves. That is when He spoke those immortal words, "Is it not written, My house shall be called of all nations the house of prayer? but ye have made it a den of thieves" (Mark 11:17).

That evening Jesus and His disciples left Jerusalem, and it was the next morning after their departure when they saw something strange. "And in the morning, as they passed by, they saw the fig tree dried up from the roots. And Peter calling to remembrance saith unto him, Master, behold, the fig tree which thou cursedst is withered away" (Mark 11:20-21).

It was a tree that had received orders or direct communication from Jesus, who has all power in heaven and in earth. Jesus spoke simply but with authority.

Communication needs to be such in each of our lives. It is said that precise communication becomes vitally important between tower and cockpit at the airport. A controller is forbidden to tell a pilot to "hold for takeoff." The mere mention of "takeoff" could trigger a response in the mind of the pilot and cause him to throw the throttles open prematurely. The correct command: "Taxi into position and hold." Because lives are at stake communication is vital.

It is the same in everyday life; the destiny of lives is determined by words that are spoken. Relationships are determined by spoken words. Speaking positive is imperative for healthy, optimistic living. We must learn to speak well!

JESUS ALWAYS SPOKE

When Jesus saw a need, He was moved with compassion but did not remain silent. He spoke. He changed things by what He spoke.

Jesus spoke to the demons:

Mark 9:25: "When Jesus saw that the people came running together, he rebuked the foul spirit, saying unto him, Thou dumb and deaf spirit, I charge thee, come out of him, and enter no more into him."

Jesus spoke to the winds:

Matthew 8:26-27: "And he saith unto them, Why are ye fearful, O ye of little faith? Then he arose, and rebuked the winds and the sea; and there was a great calm. But the men marvelled, saying, What manner of man is this, that even the winds and the sea obey him!"

Jesus spoke to the spirit of infirmity:
Luke 13:12: "And when Jesus saw her, he called her to him, and said unto her, Woman, thou art loosed from thine infirmity."

Jesus spoke to dead people:
John 11:43: "And when he thus had spoken, he cried with a loud voice, Lazarus, come forth."
Mark 5:39-41: "And when he was come in, he saith unto them, Why make ye this ado, and weep? the damsel is not dead, but sleepeth. And they laughed him to scorn. But when he had put them all out, he taketh the father and the mother of the damsel, and them that were with him, and entereth in where the damsel was lying. And he took the damsel by the hand, and said unto her, Talitha cumi; which is, being interpreted, Damsel, I say unto thee, arise."

In both cases, the dead responded and life came back into their bodies. He spoke breath back into them.

HE TOLD US TO SPEAK TO OUR MOUNTAINS

Jesus said we could speak to our mountains and they would be gone, but who believes this and is practicing this principle? "Jesus answered and said unto them, Verily I say unto you, If ye have faith, and doubt not, ye shall not only do this which is done to the fig tree, but also if ye shall say unto this mountain, Be thou removed, and be thou cast into the sea; it shall be done" (Matthew 21:21).

A mountain can represent a difficult trial, hardship,

or anything that looms before us with potential impossibilities. It would be impossible to move a mountain unless one used dynamite and bulldozers.

Jesus said that *words of faith* could act like dynamite to blow away the things that are impossible to move any other way. If Jesus said it, then it is true.

I remember and have told this story in other books, but it fits here to demonstrate the power of *words of faith*. In the 1990s a cyst was discovered in the front part of my neck. After a biopsy was performed, it swelled to the size of a small lemon underneath the skin.

I went to a ladies' retreat in Missouri and while there prayer was made for me concerning this growth. After prayer a lady minister said, "The work is done." So from that point on, when someone would ask me about my cyst, I would say, "I am healed. It is gone," even though the growth was still there.

Then in my prayer time I would speak to the cyst and tell it to dry up and leave: to go in Jesus' name! I continued to speak faith to others, and continued to speak to the cyst at odd times. I would be combing my hair and I would say, "Cyst, I command you to leave my body!"

Other times, I would be driving the car, and I would say, "I bind you, cyst, in Jesus' name, and command you to go. I loose healing into my body."

It went like this for about three months, when one day I woke up and it had disappeared. When I went back to the doctor he asked me what I had been doing, and I simply said, "We've been praying."

In the beginning of the development of this cyst, he had told me that nothing could make the cyst go away except surgery. So this was a miracle to him and for me. Matthew 21:21 and Mark 11:23 became living words to my soul: they really did work!

WE ARE TO RESIST THE DEVIL WITH WORDS

How did Jesus do this? He spoke to the devil and the devil spoke back to Him, but Jesus had the last word. The temptation came in the form of words. "And when the tempter came to him, he said, If thou be the Son of God, command that these stones be made bread" (Matthew 4:3).

Jesus answered the devil with words from the Bible: "It is written." Three times as Satan tried to beguile Jesus with words, Jesus said, "It is written," and then quoted a portion of the Holy Writ.

His final answer: "Then saith Jesus unto him, Get thee hence, Satan: for it is written, Thou shalt worship the Lord thy God, and him only shalt thou serve. Then the devil leaveth him" (Matthew 10-11a).

We are promised that the devil will also leave us when we resist him: "Resist the devil, and he will flee from you" (James 4:7).

Jesus gave example how to resist the devil and it was not through physical power, but it was through speaking the Word of God and then telling him to leave you alone. He will leave. It is promised in the Word.

In order to have this kind of power, there is the first part of verse 7 that must be obeyed: "Submit yourselves therefore to God." Then the power comes to resist the devil through speaking to him with God-given authority.

Jesus said in John 14:30: "for the prince of this world cometh, and hath nothing in me."

Arthur T. Pierson's comments on this verse are noteworthy: "Every child of God ought to be able to look the devil squarely in the face and say: 'You have nothing in me—no territory over which I acknowledge your dominion—none over my tongue, none over my temper, none over my will. You do not control me by greed; you do not control me by selfishness; you do not control me by worldliness. I am the Lord's property. Be gone, thou seducer and tempter!' Dispute him right on the border of your life over which he knows he has no control, if that life of yours is wholly God's."[2]

A powerful story is told of how God worked Easter Sunday at a church in Western Tanzania. The Ibuga Christians had to meet outdoors because the buildings could not accommodate the people who attended. While they sang and worshiped, they had no idea of the calamity that was striking their neighborhood.

About the time they started their service, a huge lioness came from the forest wild and mad. Normally a lion would kill and eat, but she was only bent on killing. She dashed from house to house attacking everything in her path. She killed three goats, a cow, and then a woman and her child. As the cry of anguish arose, the lioness ran off in the direction of the Ibuga church meeting. The villagers said that now the "Mungu Mwena" ("God is good") people will get it, for that lioness is headed directly for them.

"The congregation suddenly saw the creature only a few yards away. She stopped and growled furiously. The people quivered with shock! The preacher shouted, 'Folks, don't be afraid, the God who saved Daniel from the lions is here. The risen Christ of Easter is here.' Then with a God-given faith and authority he turned to the lioness and said, 'You lion, I curse you in the Name of Jesus Christ!'

"Then the most amazing thing happened. From the scattered clouds, though there had been no rain—nor was there any later—a bolt of lightning struck the lioness and she dropped dead in her tracks. The preacher ran and jumped up and down on the carcass and then used it as a platform to preach!"[3]

All power is in the name of Jesus and at the mention of that name the devils tremble. It is one of the most powerful weapons of the Spirit for a Christian to use.

Ephesians 1:21 describes the power of that name: "Far above all principality, and power, and might, and dominion, and every name that is named, not only in this world, but also in that which is to come."

The name of Jesus is above principality, powers, dominion of kingdoms, and every name in the heavens and the earth. It is powerful and our enemy is terrified of it.

When growing up we used to sing in church a song entitled, "In the Name of Jesus." The power of it is still the same today.

> *In the name of Jesus, in the name of Jesus,*
> *We have the victory.*
> *In the name of Jesus, In the name of Jesus,*
> *Demons will have to flee.*
> *Tell me who can stand before Him?*
> *When we go in His great name!*

Speak Something into Existence

If you want something to be removed as discussed above you can speak to it in faith and it must go. Also if you need a miracle, or you need something to come into existence, you must speak it in prayer with faith in your heart. You can have whatever you say.

Notice in the following two verses of the psalm of David that the desire of the king's heart was expressed through the speaking of his lips. Notice also that he received what he had spoken.

> *Thou hast given him his heart's desire, and hast not withholden the request of his lips. He asked life of thee, and thou gavest it him.*
> —Psalm 21:2, 4

This concept was true in the life of the prophet Elijah. After the contest on the mountain with the prophets of Baal, Elijah spoke a word that was ridiculous to the carnal ear. There had been no rain for three years, but God told Elijah that he would send rain: "And it came to pass after many days, that the word of the Lord came to Elijah in the third year, saying, Go, shew thyself unto Ahab; and I will send rain upon the earth" (I Kings 18:1).

So Elijah sent for the prophets of Baal and told them to come and see who served the true God. He wanted to demonstrate the power of His God and give them a chance to show what they could do. In the end he was the only one able to pray fire down from heaven.

After this he went and did what God told him to do: "And Elijah said unto Ahab, Get thee up, eat and drink; for

_____WHAT YOU SAY IS WHAT YOU GET_____

there is a sound of abundance of rain" (I Kings 18:41).

He spoke it before it happened because of a word from God. Then he went to pray. Elijah went to the top of Mount Carmel and put his face between his knees and prayed. He told his servant to go look at the sky. Each time he came back saying, "There is nothing."

On the seventh time, the servant said, "I see a cloud the size of a man's hand." The rain came just as Elijah had spoken. It did not come at once, but he kept praying until he saw a sign and that was enough for Elijah.

"As thou has spoken" came to pass that day!

This was proven true in the life of Moses. He spoke to the Lord that he wanted to know Him and to find grace in His sight. Exodus 33:17 gives the Lord's answer to Moses: "And the LORD said unto Moses, I will do this thing also that thou hast spoken."

We must speak it before it happens!

POWER IN THE SPOKEN WORD

It is hard for some people to believe that there is power in the spoken word. Even Moses, the great leader and deliverer of the Israelite people, found it difficult to believe this. While they were wandering in the desert they came to Kadesh and there was no water. They were hot, thirsty and murmured against Moses, who went to God with his problem. This story is recorded in Numbers 20:7-12:

And the LORD spake unto Moses, saying, Take the rod, and gather thou the assembly together, thou, and Aaron thy brother, and speak ye unto the rock before their eyes; and

> *it shall give forth his water, and thou shalt bring forth to them water out of the rock: so thou shalt give the congregation and their beasts drink. And Moses took the rod from before the LORD, as he commanded him. And Moses and Aaron gathered the congregation together before the rock, and he said unto them, Hear now, ye rebels; must we fetch you water out of this rock? And Moses lifted up his hand, and with his rod he smote the rock twice: and the water came out abundantly, and the congregation drank, and their beasts also. And the LORD spake unto Moses and Aaron, Because ye believed me not, to sanctify me in the eyes of the children of Israel, therefore ye shall not bring this congregation into the land which I have given them.*

God honored Moses because of his leadership position, but Moses only received a small portion of what he could have had, simply because he refused to speak to a rock. First of all, he was angry with the people. Maybe his anger caused him to hit the rock instead of speaking to it. Or maybe Moses did not want to be embarrassed in front of all the people by speaking to a rock. After all, what would you think if your pastor spoke to a rock and told it to send forth a river of water? Maybe Moses was not willing to be vulnerable in the eyes of the people. "What if it does not work?" he may have thought. "Then I really would have a problem." No one would think it strange to hit a rock. Moses was angry, so he struck the rock.

The Old Testament records that God told Moses to speak to a rock. The New Testament records that Jesus said to speak to a mountain. In Moses' case the rock was a literal rock. Jesus did not mean a literal mountain; He meant the mountainous situations that multiply before you in life. As Moses was punished for disobeying God, and did not receive his full promise, the same will be the lot of those who disobey the words spoken by Jesus. When He says speak, He means speak!

Speech Determines Your Future

The words of your mouth have control of your life. Whatever comes out of your mouth will determine your future. "He that keepeth his mouth keepeth his life: but he that openeth wide his lips shall have destruction" (Proverbs 13:3).

"Whoso keepeth his mouth and his tongue keepeth his soul from troubles" (Proverbs 21:23). What you say is what you get!

James likened the tongue to a rudder on a ship. The rudder controls the direction of the ship; the tongue controls the direction of your life.

Consider the bit in the horse's mouth. The bit is likened to the tongue. The bit controls the horse's actions and directions he receives for wherever he is going. Likewise, the tongue directs a person's life. The psalmist David prayed the following prayer: "I said, I will take heed to my ways, that I sin not with my tongue: I will keep my mouth with a bridle" (Psalm 39:1).

No one else can ride the racing horse of passion and tumultuous thoughts that rear and buck within you. You are the only person to hold the reins and the bridle of your tongue. The bridle consists of the leather configuration that fits over the horse including the bit and the reins. The reins control the bit in the mouth of the horse, and that in turn controls the direction of the horse.

You are sitting on life, experiencing life, and in your hands you hold the power to bridle your tongue, and you are the only one who can do it. It is a must to make this a priority and to work at getting control over the tongue. The wrong words spoken can literally cause the mind to go through torture. This is summarized in the following poem:

> "BRIDLE YOUR TONGUE"
> *That speech—it hadn't been gone half a minute*
> *Before I saw the cold black poison in it;*
> *And I'd have given all I had, and more,*
> *To've only safely got it back indoor.*
> *I'm now what most folks "Well-to-do" would call*
> *I feel today as if I'd give it all,*
> *Provided I through fifty years might reach*
> *And kill and bury that half-minute speech.*
> *Boys flying kites haul in their white-winged birds,*
> *You can't do that when you're flying words.*
> *Careful with fire—is good advice we know:*
> *Careful with words—is ten times doubly so.*
> *Thoughts unexpressed may sometimes fall back dead,*
> *But God Himself can't kill them when they're said.*
> —WILL CARLETON[4]

Instead of letting our tongues flap in any direction, we need to have control over what we say. Therefore, we will save ourselves and others from hurt and pain. Speech is forever. It cannot be erased. Once it is gone, it flies like a bird into the air. The atmosphere pulsates with our words.

Life is hard enough without putting ourselves in misery by what we speak. Attention must be given to this very important area. To stop, think, and listen should be paramount in our communication with other people.

Since we are the only one who is in control of our speech, we need to speak the things that bring faith, health and happiness as stated in the following poem:

"Talk Happiness"
Talk happiness. *The world is sad enough*
  Without your woe. No path is wholly rough;
Look for the places that are smooth and clear,
  And speak of those, to rest the weary ear
Of earth, so hurt by one continuous strain
  Of human discontent and grief and pain.

Talk faith. *The world is better off without*
  Your uttered ignorance and morbid doubt.
If you have faith in God, or man, or self,
  Say so. If not, push back upon the shelf
Of silence, all your thoughts, till faith shall come:
  No one will grieve because your lips are dumb.

Talk health. *The dreary, never-ending tale*
  Of mortal maladies is more than stale.
One cannot charm, or interest, or please
  By harping on that minor chord, disease.

Say you are well, or all is well with you,
And God shall hear your words and make them true.
—Ella Wheeler Wilcox[5]

Since speech determines our destiny and God is listening to every word we speak, we should be very careful of speaking anything that would displease Him. He has all power in heaven and in earth and if we speak the right words, powerful forces begin to work in our behalf.

The following story shares this truth: "Dr. John Baillie made it a practice to open his course on the doctrine of God at Edinburgh University with these words: 'Gentlemen, we must remember that in discussing God we cannot talk about Him without His hearing every word we say. We may be able to talk to our fellows, as it were, behind their backs, but God is everywhere, yes, even in this classroom. Therefore, in all of our discussions we must be aware of His infinite presence and talk about Him, as it were, before His face.'"[6]

"THINKING HAPPINESS"

Think of the things that make you happy,
    Not the things that make you sad;
Think of the fine and true in mankind,
    Not its sordid side and bad;
Think of the blessings that surround you,
    Not the ones that are denied;
Think of the virtues of your friendships,
    Not the weak and faulty side;

Think of the gains you've made in business,
    Not the losses you've incurred;
Think of the good of you that's spoken,
    Not some cruel, hostile word;
Think of the days of health and pleasure,
    Not the days of woe and pain;
Think of the days alive with sunshine,
    Not the dismal days of rain;

Think of the hopes that lie before you,
    Not the waste that lies behind;
Think of the treasures you have gathered,
    Not the ones you've failed to find;
Think of the service you may render,
    Not of serving self alone;
Think of the happiness of others,
    And in this you'll find your own!

—Robert E. Farley[7]

2

SPEECH: LANGUAGE OF THE SOUL

The poetic phrase, "My tongue is the pen of a ready writer," verifies this particular chapter title. The verse quoted from reveals the connection between the heart and the tongue: "My heart is inditing a good matter: I speak of the things which I have made touching the king: my tongue is the pen of a ready writer" (Psalm 45:1).

It was the heart doing the writing through the language that the tongue spoke. Speech is a gift and is the expression of the soul or the inner person.

BEAUTY OF LANGUAGE

"There is a beauty of language, just as there is a beauty of face. There is a harmony of words, just as there is a harmony of sky and stars, green foliage, and crystal waters. There is a delicacy of speech, just as there is a delicacy of tints in the masterpiece on canvas, in the shimmer of light on the dewdrop, in the semi-transparent petal of the woodland flower."[8]

Whoever is able to master the art of speaking beautifully has accomplished much. The minister who counsels a frustrated man with words of comfort so that the man leaves refreshed and with hope: that is beautiful! A nurse who whispers comforting words to a fearful patient and causes her to relax and feel protected: that is beautiful! A mother who speaks words that calm the heart of a tense child and takes away the feelings of hopelessness: that is beautiful!

Around the world people speak in different languages, but the message is the same. Everyone needs hope, comfort, advice, and reinforcement. The person who is able to give these things through the beauty of language is successful!

To heighten the usage of the beauty of language in each of us, we need to work at having beautiful thoughts as so ably penned in the following paragraph by Bertha Bailey. "The thought that is beautiful is the thought to cherish. The word that is beautiful is worthy to endure. The act that is beautiful is eternally and always true and right. Only beware that your appreciation of beauty is just and true; and to that end, I urge you to live intimately with beauty of the highest type, until it has become a part of you, until you have within you that fineness, that order, the calm, which puts you in tune with the finest things of the universe, and which links you with that spirit that is the enduring life of the world."[9]

WORDS MOVE PEOPLE

Books are filled with women and men who have influenced history with the beauty of language. Chosen words wielded together with passion, emotion, deep meaning, and honesty helped to form what penetrated deep within the hearts of the people. The power of their words changed the course of history. As an example portions of some of the famous speeches are quoted below:

Winston Churchill: German troops marched into Poland on September 1, 1939. On September 3, Great Britain and France declared war on Germany. In May of 1940 Winston Churchill at the age of sixty-six became prime minister of Great Britain. He wrote later, "I felt as if I were walking with destiny, and all my past life had been but a preparation for this hour and for this trial."

It was in June, in supreme disaster, all seemed lost and the invasion of England loomed imminent. England lay prostrate. Forty-seven warships had been sunk in the operations off Norway after Dunkirk. When the evacuation was completed, half the British destroyers were in the shipyards for repairs while the Royal Air Force had lost forty percent of its bomber strength. Britain was on the brink of famine and her armies were without arms or equipment. They had left behind in France fifty thousand vehicles.

Churchill spoke and hope was kindled in the minds of the defenseless islanders. "We shall not flag or fail, we shall go to the end, we shall fight on the seas and oceans, we shall fight with growing confidence and growing strength in the air. We shall defend our island whatever the cost may be, we shall fight on the landing grounds, we shall fight in the fields and in the streets, we shall fight in the hills; we shall never surrender, and even if, which I do not for a moment believe, this island or a large part of it were subjugated and starving, then our Empire beyond the seas, armed and guarded by the British fleet, would carry on the struggle, until, in God's good time, the New World, with all its power and might steps forth to the rescue and the liberation of the old. We will never give up! We will win."

Patrick Henry: He spoke before the Virginia Convention of Delegates on March 23, 1775. The question was independence from England. The Revolutionary War had begun and Henry said, "Is life so dear, or peace so sweet, as to be purchased at the price of chains and slavery? Forbid it! Almighty God! I know not what course others may take, but as for me, give me liberty or give me death."

Abraham Lincoln: On March 4, 1865, on the President's second inauguration, the great crowd fell silent as he stepped forward to make his address. "On the occasion corresponding to this four years ago, all thoughts were anxiously directed to an impending civil war. . . . Neither party expected for the war the magnitude or the duration which it has already attained." He continued speaking and closed with this passage which has been called, "the purest gold of human eloquence":

"With malice toward none; with charity for all; with firmness in the right, as God gives us to see the right, let us strive on to finish the work we are in; to bind up the nation's wounds; to care for him who shall have borne the battle, and for his widow and his orphan—to do all which may achieve and cherish a just and lasting peace among ourselves and with all nations."

Martin Luther King, Jr.: "I have a dream that one day every valley shall be exalted, and every hill and mountain shall be made low; the rough places will be made plain, and the crooked places will be made straight; and the glory of the Lord shall be revealed, and all flesh shall see it together.

"This is our hope. This is the faith that I go back to the South with. With this faith we will be able to hew out of the mountain of despair a stone of hope. With this faith we will be able to transform the jangling discords of our nation into a beautiful symphony of brotherhood. With this faith we will be able to work together, to pray together, to struggle together, to go to jail together, to stand up for freedom together, knowing that we will be free one day."[10]

George W. Bush: On March 27, 2002, President Bush spoke an Easter message of hope to the nation that had been devastated by the tragedy of September 11, 2001.

"During this joyful season of new life and renewal, Christians around the world celebrate the central event of their faith: the resurrection of Jesus Christ, whom Christians believe is the Messiah, the Son of God. The life and teachings of Jesus have inspired people throughout the ages to strive for a better world and a more meaningful life. Jesus' death stands out in history as the perfect example of unconditional love.

"The four Gospels of the Christian Bible recount Jesus' amazing life, his miraculous death, resurrection, and ascension, and his unending offer of salvation to all. The story of Jesus' wondrous resurrection comes alive again for Christians each year at Easter.

"Easter Sunday commemorates in song and celebration the joy and promise of Christ's triumph over evil and death. Christians around the world gather together to sing well-loved hymns to God's glory, remembering the signs and wonders of God's grace revealed in Jesus. And they again will hear Gospel readings such as Luke's rendering of that first Easter morning when the angel asked, 'Why do you look for the living among the dead? He is not here; He has risen!'

"Easter's message of renewal is especially meaningful now during this challenging time in our nation's history. On September 11, 2001, America suffered devastating loss. In the wake of great evil, however, Americans responded with strength, compassion, and generosity. As we fight to promote freedom around the world and to protect innocent lives in America, we remember the call of the Battle Hymn of the Republic: 'As He died to make men holy, let us live to make men free.'"

GUARD THE TONGUE OF THE SOUL

It has been said that the tongue is the control center of the body. This is mind-boggling: that such a small organ has such supremacy. It is of paramount importance that this mighty member be guarded and that much care be given to this power plant. Even more so because the tongue identifies one to its listeners as the following poem describes:

> Guard well thy tongue
> It stretches far;
> For what you say
> Tells what you are.

As the thoughts of the heart are meditated upon and enlarged upon, they will come tumbling pell-mell out of the mouth, and the words will either justify or condemn a person.

Jesus said it in Matthew 12:34, 37: "Out of the abundance of the heart the mouth speaketh. For by thy words thou shalt be justified, and by thy words thou shalt be condemned."

Justified or condemned by spoken words is a powerful truth that is often overlooked. How can words justify or condemn a person? It is because they convey what is in the heart. The mouth speaks what cannot be seen. It reveals sooner or later the activity of the inner man.

It is best to not speak ill of someone when the heart is on fire with bitterness and bad feelings. Take the matter to the *Heart Fixer* and give it to Him before venting the poison on someone else. Often if this is not done, there are sad consequences as the following story depicts:

"A woman, highly agitated, came into a pastor's study. She instantly began to speak abusively of a mutual acquaintance that had just been in conversation by phone with the pastor. He had failed, however, to put the receiver properly back into its cradle and his phone was still connected with the phone of the abused woman. And so she heard the terrible things that were said about her to the pastor. This incident was the beginning of an intense hatred between the two women."[11]

The beauty of language was certainly not in this conversation. Words were spoken that erected walls of hatred, and no amount of words was able to tear the wall down.

There is nothing so deadly and destructive as an unbridled tongue. Neither is there anything more powerful than words that can heal as the following poem describes:

> *A careless word may kindle strife,*
> *A cruel word may wreck a life,*
> *A bitter word may hate instill,*
> *A brutal word may smite and kill.*
> *A gracious word may smooth the way,*
> *A joyous word may light the day.*
> *A timely word may lessen stress,*
> *A loving word may heal and bless.*[12]

Govern the lips as if they were palace doors, the king within; tranquil and fair and courteous be all words which from that presence win.

—SIR EDWIN ARNOLD

SPEAK GOOD WORDS TO THE SOUL

Since speech is the language of the soul it is imperative to speak *good* words to the soul or the inner person as spoken of in the following psalm:

Speech: Language of the Soul

> *Bless the LORD, O my soul: and all that is within me, bless his holy name. Bless the LORD, O my soul, and forget not all his benefits.*
> —Psalm 103:1-2

The soul must receive good words in order to digest them into the fiber of the person. This in turn will affect the speech. The wise man said, "Excellent speech becometh not a fool" (Proverbs 17:7). Everyone must make a choice: to have or not to have excellent speech.

The tongue of a wise person has been likened to several things as shown in the following scriptures:

- "The tongue of the just is as choice silver: the heart of the wicked is little worth. The lips of the righteous feed many: but fools die for want of wisdom" (Proverbs 10:20-21).
  CHOICE SILVER
- "A word fitly spoken is like apples of gold in pictures of silver" (Proverbs 25:11).
  GOLD APPLES / SILVER PICTURES
- "A wholesome tongue is a tree of life: but perverseness therein is a breach in the spirit" (Proverbs 15:4).
  TREE OF LIFE

The tongue of the wise is very valuable, rich, and gives life. The tongue of the wicked and foolish is worthless and spreads death.

Wise people speak with a positive message. Their

tongue is likened to a tree of life or the best silver; not silver plated, but pure silver.

The tongue of the wise or the tongue of the fool is referred to often in the Scriptures. He who chooses to train himself to speak positive words that build and inspire others is a wise person.

May the first part of this scripture describe you, the reader: "The tongue of the wise useth knowledge aright: but the mouth of fools poureth out foolishness" (Proverbs 15:2).

The tongue of the wise—there is a difference and it is a difference worth seeking after and working toward.

You Speak What You Think or Believe!

You cannot rise higher than what you think and speak. Proverbs 23:7: "As [a man] thinketh in his heart, so is he."

People cannot be one thing and say another thing for very long. Sooner or later they will cross themselves up and the truth of what they are will pour forth from their mouth.

The emotions, beliefs, and passions will pour from their mind into another mind from the dam of thoughts within. There is a flow from one human being to another of feelings, impressions, principles, and attitudes.

These cannot be hid. They are the adornments of the body. A person wears them the same as they wear clothing. It is part of the nature of a person; therefore, whatever is bottled up inside will be spoken or conveyed in some way or another.

If it is doubt then doubt will manifest itself, but if it is faith, then faith will speak as stated in II Corinthians 4:13: "We having the same spirit of faith, according as it is written, I believed, and therefore have I spoken; we also believe, and therefore speak."

A person speaks what they believe, whether positive or negative, fear or courage, doubt or faith. Psalm 116:10a proved this: "I believed, therefore have I spoken."

WORDS COMMUNICATE THOUGHTS

From the beginning of time, words have been the mode of communication used to transmit a thought or idea. The following words are famous and were the first words spoken after a great event or of great consequence:

- *"What hath God wrought?"* First long-distance message by Morse telegraph.
- *"Mr. Watson, come here, I want you."* First intelligible words sent by telephone.
- *"That's one small step for man; one giant leap for mankind."* First words from astronaut Neil Armstrong as he stepped onto the moon's surface.
- *"Where art thou?"* First words spoken by God to Adam and Eve after they had sinned (Genesis 3:9).

Not all words are famous. There are words spoken daily around the world that are commonplace and are used to articulate just normal everyday thoughts and feelings.

Misunderstandings occur often between people all because of a lack of knowing how to communicate soul thoughts. It is necessary to be able to verbalize properly what one is thinking in order to help keep smooth relationships.

Some words should not be verbalized. They should be repented of and put under the blood of Jesus Christ. To sin with the lips is because of a heart condition. That is why Psalm 119:11 must be adhered to: "Thy word have I hid in mine heart, that I might not sin against thee."

In order to communicate thoughts into good words that heal, uplift, and bless, there must first be the knowledge of a Word that is higher than our thoughts and words: that is the Word of God. If everyone would seek to put this authoritative Word in their heart, there would be much less hurt, confusion, and misunderstanding.

The Right Words are Important

There are words used in certain countries that when used in other countries, have a totally different meaning as demonstrated in the story below told by Peter R. Joshua:

> "In the autumn of 1923 I arrived from Wales, my native land, with the party of David Lloyd George, famed British Prime Minister. I soon found myself the guest of the African Inland Missionary Home in Brookline, a guest who was a very lonely and homesick young man. A large group of retired lady missionaries, sensing my loneliness, arranged an afternoon tea to help dispel my gloom. At the close I was asked to say a word to the assembled ladies, and looking them squarely in the face I exclaimed, 'What language

is there to describe my gratitude to you dear women for all this kindness? What word can describe my feelings?'

"Then in a burst of enthusiasm I thundered, 'I know just the word, you are without doubt the most homely women I have ever met.' Brother, I learned the hard way that there are words used in the old country that are never used here, even if homely in Wales does mean wholesome, gracious, kind, loving and motherly."[13]

Not only do words transmit thoughts, but the choice of words is important. The same thing can be said several different ways and mean the same thing, but be more acceptable to the hearer as shown in the following story told by Clyde N. Parker:

"Once a king dreamed that all his teeth had fallen out. Immediately he sent for one of his soothsayers to interpret the meaning of the vision. With a sad countenance and mournful voice, the soothsayer told the monarch that the dream meant that all his relatives would die and that he would be left alone. This angered the king and he drove the servant from his presence.

"Another was called and the king told him of the dream. At this, the wise man smiled, and replied, 'Rejoice, O King; the dream means that you will live yet many years. In fact you will outlive all your relatives.' This pleased the king a great deal and in his joy he gave the interpreter a rich reward. The two men had said, in different ways, the same thing."[14]

Proverbs 16:13 proved to be true that day: "Righteous lips are the delight of kings; and they love him that speaketh right."

WORDS HAVE TONES

The right words are very important as this book is emphasizing, but also just as significant is the *tone* of voice in which the words are spoken.

Musical scores rely on different tones to help portray a feeling or message. It is the same way with the human voice, which is an instrument also, and is able to express tones of feeling and emotion. The right tone is almost as important as the word and sometimes more important. If someone is not able to communicate with the right words, often the tone used in the less than perfect words will convey what the heart is saying.

In compiling his book of poems, A. L. Alexander has included the following poem and made comments on this subject which will help portray what is meant by the *tone* of voice:

> "There is no power of love so hard to get and keep as a kind voice. Watch it day by day as a pearl of great price, for it is worth more than the finest pearl hid in the sea. A kind voice is to the heart like light is to the eye. It is a light that sings as well as shines."

SPEECH: LANGUAGE OF THE SOUL

"THE TONE OF VOICE"

It's not so much what you say
As the manner in which you say it;
It's not so much the language you use
As the tone in which you convey it;
"Come here!" I sharply said,
And the child cowered and wept.
"Come here," I said—
He looked and smiled
And straight to my lap he crept.
Words may be mild and fair
And the tone may pierce like a dart;
Words may be soft as the summer air
But the tone may break my heart;
For words come from the mind
Grow by study and art—
But tone leaps from the inner self
Revealing the state of the heart.
Whether you know it or not,
Whether you mean or care,
Gentleness, kindness, love, and hate,
Envy, anger, are there.
Then, would you quarrels avoid
And peace and love rejoice?
Keep anger not only out of your words—
Keep it out of your voice.

—AUTHOR UNKNOWN[15]

"Success"

Success is speaking words of praise,
In cheering other people's ways,
In doing just the best you can,
With every task and every plan,
It's silence when your speech would hurt,
Politeness when your neighbor's curt,
It's deafness when the scandal flows,
And sympathy with others' woes,
It's loyalty when duty calls,
It's courage when disaster falls,
It's patience when the hours are long,
It's found in laughter and in song,
It's in the silent time of prayer,
In happiness and in despair,
In all of life and nothing less,
We find the thing we call success.

—Author Unknown[16]

3

THE POWER OF WORDS

*Y*our words are an extension of you. The real you is your spirit. Your spirit is revealed sooner or later in what you speak. The world is spinning because of the power of words. Words are continually being spoken in all the nations of the world.

Words create an atmosphere. They form a mood or feeling; they are powerful. This is proven in the Proverbs:

> *A soft answer turneth away wrath: but grievous words stir up anger.*
> —PROVERBS 15:1

> *By long forbearing is a prince persuaded, and a soft tongue breaketh the bone.*
> —PROVERBS 25:15

Words are used to describe, persuade, motivate, enlighten, scold, praise or uplift. The list is endless. From the first words a baby utters, *ma ma* or *da da* to the last words spoken before death, words are priceless. They are the glue of society; without words communication would be difficult. How would the weatherman describe the weather? How would the diner order his dinner? How would the executive motivate his company?

Think about it. The telephone would be useless. Letters would be worthless. Books could not be. Computers would be void. Everything we do is involved with *words*.

PICTURES FROM WORDS

Words form pictures. They stimulate appetites, soothe frustrations, give directions, and even cause wars. When you look at the following list below, what does the mind visualize or what emotion is felt?

APPLE PIE
YOSEMITE
SAN FRANCISCO
MOTHER OR FATHER
CHILDHOOD
THE OLD SWIMMING HOLE
SCHOOL
TURKEY AND DRESSING
ICE CREAM
BASEBALL
CHURCH
THE BIBLE

Everyone who reads the list probably would have a different story to tell about each one. Emotions, experiences and memories evoked would differ considerably, but everything would narrow down to one simple fact: it was a *word* or *words* that brought everything into focus.

POWER OF WORDS

History will verify that *speech* is one of the greatest weapons of conflict. Hitler was able to drive the German people to an unprecedented war pitch by the power of his oratory. Other men, his superiors mentally and every other way, were unable to stop him. Why? One of the primary reasons was their inability to communicate themselves to the people. Those who were able to communicate and oppose Hitler were his most dangerous enemies. Martin Niemoller raised his voice against Hitler and, by the power of his oratory, won many of the German people.

Walter B. Knight writes his appraisal of the power of words concerning Hitler in the following paragraphs:

> It staggers the mind to try to appraise the power of words, either for good or evil. In the momentous, fateful days, when Nazism was in its nascent stage, Hitler spoke to a group of people in a beer cellar in Munich. His inflammatory words, which bristled with hate, were mirrored in the hardened faces of the evil group, and soon they engulfed the world in war.
>
> An artist has portrayed the scene, putting on canvas the facial reactions of the group to Hitler's fiery words. He gave this title to the painting: "In the Beginning Was the Word."

What a blasphemous distortion of John's words which referred to the Prince of Peace, who came not to destroy life, but that all might have life through faith in His Name.[17]

Many have said that Franklin D. Roosevelt carried the presidential election of the United States four consecutive times because he swayed the listeners with his speech.

There is power in the spoken word! For example: When Ben-hadad, king of Syria, gathered his army and went up and besieged Samaria, there was great famine and no food in the city. One of the women said to another woman, "Give your son that we may eat him today, and we will eat my son tomorrow." A horrible plight of affairs!

After boiling the son and eating him, the next day the other woman hid her son and would not give him to be eaten. When the king heard about this, he tore his clothes and put on sackcloth.

Into this scenario walked the prophet Elisha. What did he do? He spoke. "Then Elisha said, Hear ye the word of the LORD; Thus saith the LORD, To morrow about this time shall a measure of fine flour be sold for a shekel, and two measures of barley for a shekel, in the gate of Samaria" (II Kings 7:1).

Someone answers this prophecy. Words are spoken: "Then a lord on whose hand the king leaned answered the man of God, and said, Behold, if the LORD would make windows in heaven, might this thing be?"

What happened? More words are spoken. Elisha answered the sarcastic words of the doubting man:

"Behold, thou shalt see it with thine eyes, but shalt not eat thereof" (II Kings 7:2).

Words spoken by a prophet of God, words spoken by a listener, what would happen with these words? God listens to our words (especially the ones that have to do with His Word), and He does not forget them.

The end of the story: "And the people went out, and spoiled the tents of the Syrians. So a measure of fine flour was sold for a shekel, and two measures of barley for a shekel, according to the word of the LORD" (II Kings 7:16).

What happened to the lord who spoke doubt? "And the king appointed the lord on whose hand he leaned to have the charge of the gate: and the people trode upon him in the gate, and he died, as the man of God had said, who spake when the king came down to him" (II Kings 7:17). *His words caused him to be killed*!

INNER WORDS

Words that are spoken inwardly are often the most powerful words spoken. They portray the real person, motive, or results. This is proven in the story of the woman who suffered with a disease for twelve long years. She had been to many physicians, had spent all her money, but grew steadily worse. Until one day she heard of a healer called Jesus. Once when He was passing through her town, "She said within herself, If I may but touch his garment, I shall be whole" (Matthew 9:21).

It was the power of the words she spoke to herself, her inner conviction that she would be healed, that caused her to be healed. Jesus acknowledged this when He said, "Daughter, be of good comfort; thy faith hath made thee whole. And the woman was made whole from that hour" (Matthew 9:22).

That is why the words spoken to the inner self are very important. Everyone speaks to themselves in their mind. These words (the words spoken to yourself) are often the words that other people hear when verbally spoken.

Hannah of the Old Testament spoke words inside of her when she was at a desperation point in her life. "Now Hannah, she spake in her heart; only her lips moved, but her voice was not heard" (I Samuel 1:13). What was Hannah doing? She was praying to God. "And she was in bitterness of soul, and prayed unto the LORD, and wept sore" (I Samuel 1:10). Hannah was praying for a son. She was barren without any children and her life became miserable because of the taunts of another woman.

Her *heart* words were powerful! God answered her prayer. "Wherefore it came to pass, when the time was come about after Hannah had conceived, that she bare a son, and called his name Samuel, saying, Because I have asked him of the LORD" (I Samuel 1:20).

This happened more recently, in the last few years, to a little boy who refused to accept a doctor's diagnosis. Dr. Glenn Cunningham was told, as a child, that his lifeless legs would never walk or run after being burned severely. The doctors at first said he would be a vegetable, and then they said he would never walk. He would not believe what he was told, but determined that he would walk. He worked day after day, dragging himself around his yard supported by the white picket fence. He did this until he was finally able to take a few faltering steps. God looked down from heaven and saw his determination and gave him what he believed. Glenn Cunningham not only believed, but he worked at something that seemed totally impossible. Because of this he not only was able to walk again, but eventually he ran the world's fastest mile.

Inner words dictate and give signals to the body and mind on how to act, what to expect, and give direction in given situations. These inner words can be powerful or destructive depending on what is spoken inside.

WORDS THAT ABUSE

Words spoken aloud can also be powerful or destructive. There is a deadly disease that is running rampant in many homes today. It is called *verbal abuse*. The object of the abuse is often a child or a wife. It is debilitating to the nervous system of the one being abused. People wear scars all through their life simply through the negative power of words that were and are being spoken to them.

A beautiful wife under the constant barrage of belittling words from her husband often develops low self-esteem, while hiding a broken heart. She longs for words of approval, positive words of support and demonstrative love, but all she gets is caustic, hateful, and ugly words that are like bullets from a gun. They wound her spirit and soul, just as a bullet wounds the flesh. Some people die from bullet injuries; other people die from verbal stabs.

A child who is told repeatedly the following things will have to deal all their life with the power of negative words:

"You're stupid!"
"You little brat!"

"I wish you'd never been born!"
"Why can't you be more like your sister or brother?"
"You little devil, come here!"
"Here comes trouble!"
"You make me sick!"
"I can't stand you sometimes!"
"What's wrong with you? Why can't you learn?"

The list is much longer, but the hurt lasts longer. Children are sensitive and impressionable. Experts say the first seven years of a child's life are the most important years, and that they learn more in those years than in a lifetime. Many children are *branded* during those formative years, or programmed to fit into a certain category.

If children are told often enough that they are stupid, they will begin to have doubts about their intellect. Many of them begin to believe what they are told. There is one mother who would not allow her son to be branded in such a way. When she was told by the teacher that her son was *addled*, and that he could not teach him, that mother marched down to that schoolhouse and told the teacher that her son had more intelligence in his little finger than the teacher had in his whole head. She said, "If you can't teach him, I will!"

She began to teach Thomas Edison, and the world became the benefactors of the result. We need more mothers like this.

The Power of a Good Word

In Europe, Africa, the Far East, South America, Canada, America, or any other place on the earth, there _are children, churches, schools, public places, transportation and more. There are so many places where words are spoken. How many people's hearts have been warmed by a good word?

"Heaviness in the heart of man maketh it stoop: but a good word maketh it glad" (Proverbs 12:25).

I remember when my husband, our daughter and myself flew to Germany several years ago. From there we took a train to Romania where we were speaking at a conference. We met so many different people, and often we would say, "They are so kind," but there were times when we met people who were not kind.

When a person travels in a foreign country, he or she appreciates kindness and a good word, for things are strange and the language is not understandable.

We were staying at one hotel where there was a young girl who worked at the front counter. She went out of her way to help us find directions and make us feel like we were important. I still remember the lilt in her voice when she spoke.

Not only is a good word important, but also "good reports" are necessary to the human soul. We all need to be bearers of good news and look for something that we can report that will fill the hearer with joy and not dread.

"The light of the eyes rejoiceth the heart: and a good report maketh the bones fat" (Proverbs 15:30). "A good report maketh the bones fat" could be written like this: "A positive word strengthens the inner man."

Good words bring gladness; good reports bring health. Oh that there were more "good words." How many hearts have been warmed by a "word" from a caring person? How many people, who were going the wrong way, found direction by just a "word" from someone who was in touch?

In the 1990s, I remember the time when my husband and I were experiencing some tough times. It was early one morning while I was praying when the phone rang. I picked it up and I recognized the voice of a friend on the other end of the line. She began to say, "God impressed me to call and share these words with you. I found this reading in an old book that is out of print, but they are so powerful."

As she began to read, tears ran down my face, and my soul was lifted in thanksgiving to a God who knows all things, sees all things, and lays "words" on people's hearts to share with other people at just the right moment.

These were the words spoken at just the right time:

Set your gaze toward heaven. Your eyes shall behold my glory, for I have brought you through the testing time and my heart rejoices over you.

You see but a part of the picture, but I see the design in its completion. You cannot know what is in my mind and what I am creating with the material of thy life. Only be thou yielded in my hands. Thou needest not make thine own plans for I am in control, and thou wouldst bring disaster by interference, even as a child, who would wish to help a master artist and with untrained use of the brush would ruin the canvas.

So rest thy soul—this knowing that I have been at work, and in ways thou hast least suspected, for the picture and the work with which I was engaged were entirely different.

I make no idle strokes. What I do is never haphazard. My every move is one of vital creativity. And every stroke is part of the whole.

Never be alarmed by a sudden dash of color seemingly out of context. Say only in thy questioning heart, "It is the Infinite wielding His brush. Surely He doeth all things well. He can stand back and view His work and say, 'It is good.'"

"Speech of the Mind"

I wanted to affect the world and more
And walk through so many doors.
But first I had to do one thing:
Make sure of my inner king.

The one who ruled within my heart,
That secret place where I must start.
A place of information kept and stored,
Acknowledging to the world who is lord.

Our lives become known—an open book
By what we say and how we look.
For as the wind blows upon the sand,
Our speech will affect the whole of man.

Speak well today for posterity is listening;
Life moves on and is rapidly hastening.
The world waits with hushed breath;
What will we speak—life or death?

—Joy L. Haney

4

THE MIND AFFECTS SPEECH

The mind is a glorious creation created by God. The power of it is beyond man's grasp. As told in the story in Genesis about the people who had a mind that imagined they could build a tower to reach into the heavens—no one could stop them but God. If the mind has so much power, it is necessary to harness this power.

TAKE POSSESSION OF YOUR MIND

The mind can work wonders for you if you control it. It is the most powerful operating influence in your body. You are at the controls of a mighty machine that can work for you or against you. What is in the mind controls the body.

> *You are a mind with a body.*
> —W. CLEMENT STONE

Your emotions, moods, tendencies, instincts, passions, feelings, and attitudes are yours to direct. How you use them is up to you.

We are told to cast down imaginations and every high thing that exalts itself against the knowledge of God, and to bring into captivity every thought to the obedience of Christ.

This means to control the mind and the thinking process, for this controls the body. Imaginations and thoughts are to be in alignment with God's thoughts. His thoughts are creativity, success, power, magnificence, greatness, and life itself. These are the thoughts that should control our mind. If the mind is allowed to run pell-mell in any direction with no director at the controls, is it any wonder there are so many confused people.

The mind is a beautiful gift from God to be used in a positive manner. Our life consists of what our thoughts make of it. If we think happy thoughts, we will be happy. If we think miserable thoughts, we will be miserable. If we allow fear to dominate our minds, we will be fearful.

Norman Vincent Peale had a witty way of saying it: "You are not what you think you are; but what you *think*, you are."

This is an echo of Proverbs 23:7: "For as he thinketh in his heart, so is he."

The mind is much like a garden. You dig holes in the ground and plant, say, corn. You cover the holes with dirt, water it and fertilize it. What happens? The ground will return to you exactly what was planted.

"Your conscious mind and your subconscious mind work in exactly the same way. If your conscious mind plants anger, resentment, envy, failure, defeat, and other

THE MIND AFFECTS SPEECH

negative thoughts in your subconscious mind, you will get back precisely what you have planted. As you can easily see from this example, *a person does literally become what he thinks about.*"[18]

Life has a way of revealing what we are thinking. We either are letting life use us or we are using life as Frank A. Court said it so well in the following paragraph:

"What a difference it makes when we are using life rather than having life use us. When we, to a marked degree, are managing our moods, controlling our emotions, making life meaningful, filling every day with the heights of Christian living, we may say with confidence that we are using life.

"But when worry grips the mind and paralyzes the heart, or the dull edge of sin robs life of radiancy, or fear grips our life, rather than an abiding faith, and life runs out into a morass of doubt, disillusionment and despair, we know that life is using us."[19]

What the mind thinks, the mind speaks; therefore, it is crucial to guard the mind, for the tongue is an extension of the mind.

There is an interesting phrase penned in Psalm 73:9: "Their tongue walketh through the earth." How does a tongue walk? It walks in a body. The mind controls the tongue and the mind controls the body; therefore, when a tongue is said to walk, the tongue represents the whole of a person, for the tongue reveals the mind.

KEEP YOUR MIND FOCUSED

Consciously keep your mind on the things you want and off the things you do not want to be in your mind. You must learn to discipline your thoughts and visualize the right things.

With every failure, sorrow, adversity, or unpleasant circumstance everyone has the opportunity to react in a positive manner.

No one can change the past, but anyone can affect the present and the future. Paul said to forget the past and look towards your goal. Dwelling on failures or negative feelings only makes things worse.

> *This one thing I do, forgetting those things which are behind, and reaching forth unto those things which are before.*
> —PHILIPPIANS 3:13

This does not mean that one can block out of their mind something that was a horrible experience and just go on, but something must be done. The difference is concern or worry about it. Concern is to realize what the problems are and calmly take steps to correct them or to let them go. Worry means going around in useless, maddening circles developing ulcers over something that needs to be let go or at least develop a workable solution to the problem.

Milton, the blind poet, wrote,

The mind is its own place, and in itself
Can make a heaven of Hell, a hell of Heaven.

"Napoleon and Helen Keller are perfect illustrations of Milton's statement: Napoleon had everything men usually crave—glory, power, riches—yet he said at Saint Helena, 'I have never known six happy days in my life,' while Helen Keller—blind, deaf, dumb—declared: 'I have found life so beautiful.'"[20]

How the Mind Works

There is the conscious mind and the subconscious mind. "Your subconscious mind does not think or act on its own volition or its own initiative. *Its primary purpose is to achieve the goals that have been given to it by your conscious mind.*"[21]

"Your conscious mind is that part of your brain that enables you to know, to think, and to act effectively. Your conscious mind uses logic, deduction, and reasoning to reach its conclusions and make its decisions. Your choices, your decisions as to what you will or will not do are made by your conscious mind, not by your subconscious mind."[22]

There are three forms of control you can exert: suggestion, self-suggestion, and autosuggestion.

Suggestion is any stimulus sent through your brain through your five senses. All of these are pathways by which external elements influence you every day. Everything you come in contact with is stored in the subconscious mind.

Self-suggestion is the process of purposely and deliberately offering stimuli to yourself in the form of seeing, hearing, feeling, tasting, or smelling. No matter what happens to you look for the good in it. Do not allow bad things to make you bitter or negative. Just accept it as a learning experience.

Repeat to yourself: "The Lord is with me. He is helping me." The more you purposely repeat a message to yourself the more it is implanted in the subconscious mind. Repeat over and over what it is you want. Say, "I feel terrific," and your body begins to respond to what you are speaking.

When you say to yourself "I can!" you motivate yourself by *self-suggestion*. Paul gave us these words to say in Philippians 4:13: "I can do all things through Christ which strengtheneth me."

Autosuggestion is the transmission and communication of information stored in the subconscious mind back to the conscious mind. The information returns in the form of ideas, feelings, principles, dreams, thoughts, etc. When you feed your mind with good thoughts and information, you are supplying the subconscious with good material to feed back to you.

CLEANSING THE MIND

Some minds are like graveyards. Pictures of disease, sickness, fear, torment, doubt, death, depression, and dismay line the corridor of the mind. There is a phrase mentioned in Ezekiel 8:12 that is very enlightening: "Every man in the chambers of his imagery."

This chamber of imaginations is what dictates to the body and life of a person. Therefore, it is necessary to do a mental cleaning of the imaginations in the mind.

The story told in Ezekiel 37 dubbed as "Ezekiel's Bone Yard" is a picture of the death inside many people. The bones said, "Our bones are dried; our hope is lost." God said, "O my people, I will open your graves, and cause

The Mind Affects Speech

you to come up out of your graves." Ezekiel 37:14 gives the secret: "[I] shall put my Spirit in you, and ye shall live."

The breath of the Spirit needs to blow into the stale corridors of the mind and cleanse us from disillusionment, fear and torment. We need to be on fire with faith and power!

After the cleansing, the walls of the corridors are scrubbed and painted with heaven's hues. Then new pictures must be hung to replace the old ones. Go to the art gallery of the Word and pick out the best pictures in the Book and order them to be hung there permanently.

You are responsible to place the order, to hang the pictures, and also to be the keeper of them to make sure they do not get dusty, dim, or destroyed. What pictures you allow to hang in the corridors of your mind are entirely up to you, but remember they will impress you, dictate to you, affect your speech and destiny.

As the mind receives information the tongue speaks of it, as demonstrated in Psalm 119:171: "My lips shall utter praise, when thou hast taught me thy statutes."

"Little Words"

"Yes, you did, too!"
"I did not!"
Thus the little quarrel started,
Thus by unkind little words,
Two fond friends were parted.

"I am sorry."
"So am I."
Thus the little quarrel ended,
Thus by loving little words
Two fond hearts were mended.

—Benjamin Keech[23]

5
ENEMIES OF SPEAKING POSITIVE

Usually anything good has its enemies. This applies to speaking positive also. Since it is a good thing, there are things that would seek to destroy in an individual the ability to speak positive. A few of these enemies are listed in this chapter. They need to be dealt with and overcome because life and death are in the power of the tongue. We must choose life today!

FEAR

Fear can cancel positive speaking if allowed to dwell in the mind.

We had a friend whose wife was known to speak these words often: "I'm afraid someday they're going to open me up and find me full of cancer." Her worst fears were realized. The day did come when after much pain in her stomach they did operate on her and found that she was filled with cancer just as she had spoken.

Proverbs 18:21 declares: "Death and life are in the power of the tongue." We can speak *life* for others and ourselves, or we can speak *death* to others and ourselves. Not only *can* we, but we *are* speaking it every day.

Fear is not of God. It is something that must be confronted and spoken to and told to leave. "God hath not given us the spirit of fear; but of power, and of love, and of a sound mind" (II Timothy 1:7).

When fear comes to visit, we must recognize that God does not want the fear to dominate, but instead for His love and power to be in control. If God is love, which He is, and if perfect love casts out fear, which it does, then it is simple understanding that recognizes that where God is, there can be no fear. So when fear comes to you, and it will, you must sit quietly and clear your mind of fear and begin to speak faith in the face of fear.

It must be realized that God is with you and that He brings love, power and soundness. He uses the opposite of fear tactics. He gives peace, joy, comfort and healing.

Speak positively in the face of negative facts. "God is with me. He is here to heal me." An excellent choice of verse to be spoken in a time of crisis is the twenty-third psalm.

> *The LORD is my shepherd; I shall not want.*
> *He maketh me to lie down in green pastures: he leadeth me beside the still waters.*
> *He restoreth my soul: he leadeth me in the paths of righteousness for his name's sake.*
> *Yea, though I walk through the valley of the shadow of death, I will fear no evil: for thou art with me; thy rod and thy staff they comfort me.*

Enemies of Speaking Positive

Thou preparest a table before me in the presence of mine enemies: thou anointest my head with oil; my cup runneth over.

Surely goodness and mercy shall follow me all the days of my life: and I will dwell in the house of the LORD for ever.

This is the day to go inside our minds and close some doors to negative emotions. Close the door on fear and doubt and go forward in the light of God's Word as the following poem describes:

"CLOSING THE DOORS"
I have closed the door on Doubt.
I will go by what light I can find,
And hold up my hands and reach them out
To the glimmer of God in the dark, and call,
"I am Thine, though I grope and stumble and fall.
I serve, and Thy service is kind."

I have closed the door on Fear
He has lived with me far too long.
If he were to break forth and reappear,
I would lift my eyes and look at the sky,
And sing aloud and run lightly by;
He will never follow a song.

I have closed the door on Gloom.
His house has too narrow a view.
I must seek for my soul a wider room,
With windows to open and let in the sun,

*And radiant lamps when the day is done,
And the breeze of the world blowing through.*
—Irene Pettit McKeehan[24]

Enter into the room of faith, for faith must triumph over fear. Believe the words of Jesus: "If ye have faith as a grain of mustard seed, ye shall say unto this mountain, Remove hence to yonder place; and it shall remove; and nothing shall be impossible unto you" (Matthew 17:20).

Ignorance

Some people speak negatively because that is all they know how to speak. They have not been enlightened on the power of speech. It is the way they were trained. They have always done it that way.

In the lips of him that hath understanding wisdom is found: but a rod is for the back of him that is void of understanding. Wise men lay up knowledge: but the mouth of the foolish is near destruction.
—Proverbs 10:13-14

People who speak without first consulting God give themselves a beating. They are self-destructing.

This happened in the case of a man named Marshall Cummings of Tulsa, Oklahoma, who was accused of purse snatching. He chose to be his own lawyer, but he was not very successful in pleading his case. As he cross-examined the victim, he asked: "Did you get a good look at my face when I took your purse?" A state jury convicted

ENEMIES OF SPEAKING POSITIVE

Cummings of attempted robbery by force and gave him a ten-year prison sentence.

He was snared by his own words. His ignorance came from the fact that his world was a shady one of dishonesty and godlessness. Because of what he was and how he lived, he was ignorant of the higher road of living and it affected his speech. He chose this road of darkness where there was no light.

Our lifestyles, attitudes, and what we speak reflects what we know. If someone does not know any better, then that is understandable, but if someone knows to live a better life and to speak positive faith, and refuses to do so, they live in ignorant darkness.

There are some who truly have not learned the right way as demonstrated in the following story. The boy's ignorance was because he had not been taught; he just did not know any better.

A little boy who was keeping sheep one Sunday morning heard the church bells ringing and saw the people going over the field to the church. He began to think that he too would like to pray to God, so he knelt by a hedge and began to pray. Since he had never learned a prayer, he began to say the alphabet: A, B, C, etc.

A gentleman happening to pass on the other side of the hedge heard the boy and, looking through the bushes, saw him kneeling with folded hands saying, "A, B, C."

"What are you doing, my little man?"

"Please, sir, I was praying." "But what are you saying your letters for?" "Why, I didn't know any prayer, only I felt that I wanted God to take care of me and help me to care for the sheep; so I thought if I said all I knew, he would put it together and spell all I want."[25]

How much like this boy are some people. Not really knowing how or what to say, they let the words tumble out of their mouth hoping that the listener will be able to spell the message correctly.

The problem is that people are not God, as in the case of the little boy's listener. God can take the alphabet and spell the words that are coming from the heart, but most people cannot do this. So it behooves us all to learn to speak the right way and leave ignorance behind.

CIRCUMSTANCES

Instead of being in control of their tongues and emotions, many people allow their tongues and emotions to be controlled by what happens to them. If something good happens, they feel happy and express how they feel. If something bad happens, they feel threatened and often give in to despair, speaking negative words about what happened.

Will we allow circumstances to dictate to us how to act, or will we determine to have the right attitudes and speech? What do we wish for most—to be dashed around like a piece of driftwood in the sea or to be steadfast and firm as a rock, where the sea dashes over and around it, but does not move it?

Circumstances beyond our control demand a strong will if we are to survive victoriously as penned so beautifully in the following poem:

"WILL"
There is no chance, no destiny, no fate,
Can circumvent or hinder or control

Enemies of Speaking Positive

The firm resolve of a determined soul,
Gifts count for nothing; will alone is great;
All things give way before it, soon or late.
What obstacle can stay the mighty force
Of the sea-seeking river in its course,
Or cause the ascending orb of day to wait?
Each wellborn soul must win what it deserves:
Let the fool prate of luck. The fortunate
Is he whose earnest purpose never swerves,
Whose slightest action or inaction serves
The one great aim. Why, even Death stands still,
And waits an hour sometimes for such a will.

—Ella Wheeler Wilcox[26]

Every person in the world will experience circumstances in which they desperately wish they could push the "delete" button and they would disappear. Circumstances dictate fear, hopelessness, doubt, anger, and frustration. We must *will* ourselves to seek God until His emotions fill our being. For with God all things are possible to him that believeth. He is our strength, our hope, and the bearer of our burdens who can work out all things for His good.

It is to Him that we must look. "Come unto me, all ye that labour and are heavy laden, and I will give you rest" (Matthew 11:28). He is there for us. He will help us during the worst circumstances—those times when we feel as if all hell has broken loose against us. God is bigger than the perpetrator of evil. God has all power in heaven and in earth; therefore, choose to trust Him in the most extenuating circumstance!

UNYIELDED TONGUES

The whole person must be yielded to God and His ways in order to please Him. Romans 6:13 gives instructions about the proper way to yield: "Neither yield ye your members as instruments of unrighteousness unto sin: but yield yourselves unto God, as those that are alive from the dead, and your members as instruments of righteousness unto God."

James 3:5-6 identifies our tongue as a member: "Even so the tongue is a little member, and boasteth great things. Behold, how great a matter a little fire kindleth! And the tongue is a fire, a world of iniquity: so is the tongue among our members, that it defileth the whole body, and setteth on fire the course of nature; and it is set on fire of hell."

The tongue of a shoe is the piece of leather that is pliable and is able to flap back and forth. The tongue of a wagon hooks onto the back of a truck. The tongue is the thing that joins itself to other things. We need to make sure we join our tongues to a God-controlled mind so that we speak as oracles of God and not of the carnal nature.

> "Unless we yield our tongues as instruments of righteousness unto God, Satan will use them to his advantage, and to our spiritual impoverishment. Some people pride themselves that they have the gift of gab. But one thing is certain—what little spirituality such people possess may soon dribble away via the mouth."
>
> —WALTER B. KNIGHT[27]

May this not happen to us—dribble at the mouth, saying things with a tongue that is not under the control of or yielded to the things that make good speaking!

_____ENEMIES OF SPEAKING POSITIVE_____

A FORKED TONGUE

To speak out of both sides of the mouth is the surest way to be a loser. A description of this type of individual is found in James 1:8: "A double minded man is unstable in all his ways."

Sometimes these kinds of people are very adept in flattery. They speak sweet, kind words to your face, but behind your back, their evil spirit causes them to speak hurtful words that intend to destroy.

Notice in the following scriptures how flattery (speaking sweet words that are insincere) are coupled with gross sins:

Psalm 5:9: "For there is no faithfulness in their mouth; their inward part is very wickedness; their throat is an open sepulchre; they flatter with their tongue."

Psalm 12:2: "They speak vanity every one with his neighbour: with flattering lips and with a double heart do they speak."

Psalm 78:36: "Nevertheless they did flatter him with their mouth, and they lied unto him with their tongues."

Proverbs 26:28: "A lying tongue hateth those that are afflicted by it; and a flattering mouth worketh ruin."

Proverbs 29:5: "A man that flattereth his neighbour spreadeth a net for his feet."

Walter Knight gives the following insight on the double talker:

> There are many words that cause Bible translators difficulty when translating them into

the languages of tribes and nations. There is one word, however, which presents no difficulty to the translators, and that word is hypocrisy. Hypocrisy is a universal sin. The hypocrite is found everywhere. The Indian tribes in Latin America have various ways to denote the hypocrite. They designate him as "a man with two faces," "a man with two hearts," "a man with two kinds of talk," "a two-headed man," "a forked-tongue person," "a two-sided man," and "a man with a straight mouth and a crooked heart."[28]

This is one sin that needs to be avoided. God desires that truth be in the inward parts of a man. If truth, kindness, and love are in the inside, then the tongue will speak the same thing to someone's face and also behind their back.

Psalm 51:6: "Behold, thou desirest truth in the inward parts: and in the hidden part thou shalt make me to know wisdom." This is what God wants for His children, and those who attain this state of being are on their way to being known as speaking positive.

BAD ATTITUDES

Bad attitudes are reflected in speech. We have all heard the phrase, "They've been eating sour grapes." It must be remembered that it is a firm commandment to put away the *sour grapes*, and not let it affect the inner person.

Psalm 140:11 declared the will of God in this matter: "Let not an evil speaker be established in the earth." May we be delivered from being that person!

Enemies of Speaking Positive

The Scriptures address evil speaking in several places:

- "Laying aside . . . all evil speakings" (I Peter 2:1).
- "To speak evil of no man, to be no brawlers, but gentle, shewing all meekness unto all men" (Titus 3:2).
- "Keep thy tongue from evil, and thy lips from speaking guile" (Psalm 34:13).
- "Let all bitterness, and wrath, and anger, and clamour, and evil speaking, be put away from you, with all malice" (Ephesians 4:31).

Bitterness is not a coat that is worn on the outside, but it is a stagnant pool of acid that has formed in the mind of someone. It pollutes the whole person, manifesting itself from time to time though a caustic and sour tongue.

When wrath [resentment, indignation], anger [rage, animosity, hostility], and clamor [uproar, disorder, chaos] have taken up permanent residence on the inside of someone, their mouth becomes the smokestack that emits the communicative residue that erupts from the boiling inferno.

It cannot be hidden forever. What is on the inside eventually comes out! The mouth is the mirror of the mind, heart and soul.

If you want God's blessing, you must first learn to speak no evil as the following verses indicate:

What man is he that desireth life, and loveth many days, that he may see good?

Power of Speaking Positive

Keep thy tongue from evil, and thy lips from speaking guile.

—Psalm 34:12, 13

Wherefore laying aside all malice, and all guile, and hypocrisies, and envies, and all evil speakings.

—I Peter 2:1

The meanest and most contemptible kind of praise is that which first speaks well of a man, and then qualifies it with a "but!"

—Henry Ward Beecher[29]

Instead of speaking evil of other people learn to speak kindly of them. Kindness is the spark that mends hearts and brings families together. We need to pray for a kind heart so we can do as the poet encourages us to do in the following poem:

"Speak Kindness"
Kind hearts are the gardens,
    Kind thoughts are the roots,
Kind words are the flowers,
    Kind deeds are the fruits.

Take care of your garden,
    And keep out the weeds;
Fill it up with sunshine,
    Kind words and kind deeds.

—Longfellow[30]

Enemies of Speaking Positive

> *Speak kind words and you will hear kind echoes.*
> —Bahn

These six enemies are listed: fear, ignorance, circumstances, an unyielded tongue, a forked tongue, and bad attitudes, but there are other enemies as well. There are always enemies fighting to get the upper hand in our lives, but the question is—who or what will we allow to win over the control center of our life? We can have *apples of gold* speech or *pictures of silver* indicating excellent speech if we desire it enough!

"Three Gates of Gold"

If you are tempted to reveal
    A tale to you someone has told
About another, make it pass,
    Before you speak, three gates of gold;
These narrow gates. First, "Is it true?"
    Then, "Is it needful?" In your mind
Give truthful answer. And the next
    Is last and narrowest, "Is it kind?"
And if to reach your lips at last
    It passes through these gateways three,
Then you may bell the tale, nor fear
    What the result of speech may be.

—Beth Day[31]

6

Train Yourself to Speak Positive

$\mathcal{A}$nyone can be trained to do something that they have never done before. It is a process: step-by-step, word-by-word, and action-by-action. The disciplines of the soul take time. The worth is immeasurable and cannot even be considered not doing. Most everyone speaks, and "According to statisticians the average person spends at least one-fifth of his or her life talking. Ordinarily, in a single day enough words are used to fill a 50-page book. In one year's time the average person's words would fill 132 books, each containing 400 pages."[32]

If a person is going to spend that much time talking, then why not be trained to speak positive?

Proverbs 16:23 says, "The heart of the wise teacheth his mouth, and addeth learning to his lips."

Whatever it is that you feed your heart and mind, this will affect your language.

Develop Positive Thoughts

In computer language there is a code called *GIGO*, which interpreted means *garbage in—garbage out*. But what about interpreting it this way: *good in—good out*. In other words, what is programmed into the mind will come out through the spoken word.

It is possible to develop positive thinking and positive speaking. Someone once said, "It is not mind over matter, but mouth over matter."

People can be trained in any area, but it takes time to become a specialist or a professional. If someone wants to learn the piano, there is a process involved. There is discipline, practice, and more practice. Even then it takes years to attain the desired results.

A good doctor does not evolve overnight, but after eight years of schooling, he or she is still learning to become. An artist paints many years before becoming a Van Gogh. In so many areas people are willing to train, work, practice, sacrifice, and study in order to become an expert in their particular line of work. But how many people are willing to take the same amount of time to study, work, practice and train the mind to become a manufacturer of positive thoughts that produce positive speaking?

Becoming a positive speaker does not happen overnight. It takes time, fine-tuning, and discipline. Those who want to speak positive and create positive things must first be prepared to delete that which would defeat their purpose.

The oldest book of wisdom gives the formula for beginning to think in a positive manner. It instructs one to think on things that are true, that are honest, that are just and pure, lovely, of good report and that have virtue or praise, which is captured in the following poem:

TRAIN YOURSELF TO SPEAK POSITIVE

Think noble thoughts if you would noble be;
Pure thoughts will make a heart of purity;
Kind thoughts will make you good, and glad thoughts gay,
For like your thoughts your life will be always.

Whate'er is true and reverend and just
Think o'er these things, and be like them you must;
Of good report, of lovely things and pure,
Think, and your mind such nectar shall secure.

Think much of God and you shall like Him be,
In words of faith and hope and charity;
Protect His image from all foul abuse,
And keep the temple holy for His use.

—F. G. BURROUGHS

HOW TO DEVELOP POSITIVE SPEAKING

1. *PRAY EVERY MORNING.*

> *As one whose whole life has been concerned with the sufferings of the mind, I would state that of all the hygienic measures to counteract disturbed sleep, depression of spirits, and all the miserable sequels of a distressed mind, I would undoubtedly give the first place to the simple habit of prayer.*
>
> —DR. HYSLOOP[33]

My voice shalt thou hear in the morning, O LORD; in the morning will I direct my prayer unto thee, and will look up.

—PSALM 5:3

When you pray to God, His presence will be with you and He will be in your thoughts. What you speak is the voice of your thoughts. Therefore, when you rub shoulders with divinity through prayer, it is an absolute fact that your speech will be altered. When God's Spirit breathes upon you, the stale thoughts that were originally in your mind are dislodged and swept away and are replaced by thoughts of glory and splendor.

Notable words written by Joseph Park are as follows: "The morning is the time fixed for my meeting the Lord. This very word *morning* is as a cluster of rich grapes. Let me crush them, and drink the sacred wine. In the night I have buried yesterday's fatigue, and in the morning I take a new lease of energy. Blessed is the day whose morning is sanctified! Successful is the day whose first victory is won in prayer."

Pray this prayer each morning: "Set a watch, O LORD, before my mouth; keep the door of my lips" (Psalm 141:3).

There are hinges on your lips that hold a door. This door releases the secrets of the soul. If you want good things to come forth from the storehouse within you, it is good to ask the Lord to create a clean heart within you and to help guard the opening and shutting of the door.

Prayer is a time of talking and listening to God. True prayer will affect a person's speech *after* the prayer with whomever they come in contact. The following poem reflects this:

"LORD, SPEAK TO ME"
*Lord, speak to me, that I may speak
In living echoes of Thy tone;*

As Thou hast sought, so let me seek
   Thy erring children lost and lone.

O teach me, Lord, that I may teach
   The precious things Thou dost impart;
And wing my words, that they may reach
   The hidden depths of many a heart.

O fill me with Thy fullness, Lord,
   Until my very heart o'erflow
In kindling thought and glowing word,
   Thy love to tell, Thy praise to show.
—Frances Ridley Havergal[34]

Some people wonder how prayer works, and have never been fully convinced of its power. There were some men during World War II who were just like this, but after experiencing being lost in the ocean for twenty-one days and being found, they were convinced of its power.

The airplane carrying Captain Edward Rickenbacker and his crew fell into the Pacific Ocean and no trace of the wreckage could be found. There they were with three rafts, which they tied together at night, with no food except a few oranges.

Rickenbacker, who had been raised by a praying mother, knew the power of prayer. On the second day out it was found one of the boys had a Bible in his pocket. So they organized little prayer meetings during the mornings and evenings, and took turns reading passages from the Bible. They humbly prayed for their deliverance.

On the eighth day, within one hour after prayer, a sea

gull came out of nowhere and landed on Captain's head. He reached up his hand very gently and caught him. The men wrung his head, feathered him, carved up his carcass and ate every bit, even the little bones. Then they used his innards for bait. They caught several fish after that, which kept them alive.

On the twenty-first day of their ordeal, they were located by searching planes and picked up. It was a truly miraculous rescue, for the rafts were less than dots on the ocean's surface and impossible to see from a distance.

When news of the rescue was flashed around the world, people everywhere were thrilled and excited, for most people thought they were lost for good. But what moved people most was Rickenbacker's simple answer, "We prayed."

He wrote a book about their experience, *Seven Came Through*. There were originally eight men in the three tiny rubber lifeboats, which they fastened together with rope. One man died on the thirteenth day; but the other seven came safely through the ordeal. They acknowledged that their miracle was through prayer and reading of the Bible.

2. *READ THE BIBLE EVERY DAY*.

> *It is impossible to mentally or socially enslave a Bible-reading people. The principles of the Bible are the groundwork of human freedom.*
> —HORACE GREELEY[35]

Capt. Rickenbacker and his men did read the Bible every day. Can you imagine being lost in the middle of an ocean, with no food or water, no help in sight and grown men turning to divine help in the time of their need? Their voices reading the Word, mingling with the roar of the waves, got the attention of God. They chose especially two passages to read: The twenty-third psalm and the following portion from Matthew 6:

> *Therefore take no thought, saying, What shall we eat? or, What shall we drink? or, Wherewithal shall we be clothed? . . . for your heavenly Father knoweth that ye have need of all these things.*
>
> *But seek ye first the kingdom of God, and his righteousness; and all these things shall be added to you.*
>
> *Take therefore no thought for the morrow: for the morrow shall take thought for the things of itself. Sufficient unto the day is the evil thereof.*

As the Word began to penetrate the elements, the pulsating, creative power of God began to work in their behalf. Forces were put into motion because of the power of the Book. It is a fire, a light, a hammer, and oh so powerful!

The Word is the wisdom of God. As these power thoughts are assimilated into the brain, heart and mind, they become part of your vocabulary and understanding.

The Word gives light and understanding: "The entrance of thy words giveth light; it giveth understanding unto the simple" (Psalm 119:130).

The Word gives wisdom: "For the LORD giveth

wisdom: out of his mouth cometh knowledge and understanding" (Proverbs 2:6).

The following is the promise of blessing to those who seek God's wisdom:

> *So shalt thou find favour and good understanding in the sight of God and man. Trust in the LORD with all thine heart; and lean not unto thine own understanding. In all thy ways acknowledge him, and he shall direct thy paths. Be not wise in thine own eyes: fear the LORD, and depart from evil. It shall be health to thy navel, and marrow to thy bones.*
> —PROVERBS 3:4-8

The mind must be programmed with the Word of God. Psalm 119:105 states, "Thy word is a lamp unto my feet, and a light unto my path."

The Word is a lamp of understanding, showing the immediate way to go, and a light leading the way ahead of us. A mind that is filled with God's wisdom becomes the fountain of positive speaking.

The mind is the battlefield between good and evil, or negative and positive thinking. The mind becomes filled with the litter of life, the debris of depression and the sour notes of the general society. Any thought that exalts itself or becomes larger than the pure Word of God should be treated as an intruder into the inner source of power. The mind is a factory; it manufactures and produces a product. The product that is produced is introduced through the mouth, and utters whatever is silently going on inside the mind.

Train Yourself to Speak Positive

The mind must be trained to reject that which is contrary to the positive Word of God. Each individual must attend training seminars to strengthen the mind. These training seminars can be done daily in the privacy of your own home. The teacher is the Word of God. It contains wisdom that even the most gifted speaker cannot attain through the highest educational systems in the world.

Wilfred T. Grenfell, M.D. had this to say about the Word: "To me the memorizing of Scripture has been an unfailing help in doubt, anxiety, sorrow, and all the countless vicissitudes and problems of life.

"I believe in it enough to have devoted many, many hours of stowing away passages where I can neither leave them behind me or be unable to get to them.

"The Word of God is the Christian's best weapon and must be with him always. Facing death alone on a floating piece of ice on a frozen ocean, the comradeship it afforded me supplied all I needed. It stood by me like the truest of true friends that it is.

"With my whole soul I commend to others the giving of some time each day to secure the immense returns that memorizing the Word of God offers and insures."[36]

We must do this and follow the advice of Proverbs 3:5: "Lean not unto thine own understanding."

3. *Acknowledge God.*

> *We and God must have business one with the other, and in opening our hearts to Him our highest destiny is fulfilled.*
> —William James

God has influence over those who reverence Him, but not over the wicked because they refuse to seek after Him. Therefore, their *thoughts* influence their *mouth*.

> *The wicked . . . will not seek after God: God is not in all his thoughts. His mouth is full of cursing and deceit and fraud.*
> —Psalm 10:4, 7

It is promised that the Lord will cut off the wicked and those who do not acknowledge Him.

> *The Lord shall cut off all flattering lips, and the tongue that speaketh proud things: who have said, With our tongue will we prevail; our lips are our own: who is lord over us?*
> —Psalm 12:3-4

It is best to humbly ask God for help rather than try to figure things out for yourself. A good prayer to pray is the following one:

> *Let the words of my mouth, and the meditation of my heart, be acceptable in thy sight, O Lord, my strength, and my redeemer.*
> —Psalm 19:14

We are commanded to *talk* about God. "O give thanks unto the Lord; call upon his name: make known his deeds among the people. Sing unto him, sing psalms unto him: talk ye of all his wondrous works" (Psalm 105:1-2).

"O give thanks unto the Lord, for he is good: for his mercy endureth for ever. Let the redeemed of the Lord *say* so" (Psalm 107:1-2).

Decide today to join the psalmist David in his declaration: "I will speak of the glorious honour of thy majesty, and of thy wondrous works" (Psalm 145:5). "My mouth shall speak the praise of the Lord" (Psalm 145:21).

To acknowledge God and bring Him into your world is to bring magnificence into your sphere of living. He is the great, all-knowing power that was before the beginning and will be forever.

"How do you know whether there be a God?" was once asked of a Bedouin, and he replied: "How do I know whether a camel or a man passed my tent last night? By their footprints in the sand."

God's footprints are seen everywhere. Psalm 19:1 thunders it: "The heavens declare the glory of God; and the firmament sheweth his handywork."

To acknowledge God is to acknowledge His Word. Great emphasis must be placed upon the Word, for it is irrefutable and unbeatable. Nothing can win against the Word of God. When Edward VI was crowned king of England, three swords were placed before him as tokens of his power. Said the king: "Bring another sword: 'the sword of the Spirit, which is the Word of God!' I need this sword more than any other to overcome evil!"

King Edward respected God and the power of the Word. He did not want to rule his kingdom without them, and acknowledged this before all the lords of the court and men of renown. What a powerful statement!

If you have trouble acknowledging God and His

greatness, humbly repent and ask God to give you a revelation of Him, for people who say there is no God are labeled fools in Psalm 53:1: "The fool hath said in his heart, There is no God. Corrupt are they, and have done abominable iniquity: there is none that doeth good."

What does science have to say about God?

> "I have found nothing in science or space exploration to compel me to throw away my Bible or to reject my Savior, Jesus Christ, in whom I trust. The space age has been a factor in the deepening of my own spiritual life. I read the Bible more now. I get from the Bible what I cannot get from science—the really important things of life."
> —WALTER F. BURKE, SERVED AS GENERAL MANAGER OF PROJECT MERCURY AND GEMINI

> "The more I study science the more I am impressed with the thought that this world and universe have a definite design, and a design suggests a designer."
> —PAUL AMOS MOODY, SERVED AS PROFESSOR OF ZOOLOGY UNIVERSITY OF VERMONT[37]

> "No one can study chemistry and see the wonderful way in which certain elements combine with the nicety of the most delicate machine ever invented, and not come to the inevitable

conclusion that there is a Big Engineer who is running this universe."

—Thomas Edison[38]

4. Develop Habits of Praise and Thanks.

> *When we bless God for mercies, we prolong them. When we bless God for miseries, we usually end them. Praise is the honey of life which a devout heart extracts from every bloom of providence and grace.*
>
> —Spurgeon

Habits are first like cobwebs, then they become chains. We all decide what we are *chained* to: praise or grumbling, praise or criticizing, etc.

If the whole earth and the universe praise their Creator, why shouldn't mankind do the same? "Praise ye the Lord. Praise ye the Lord from the heavens: praise him in the heights. Praise ye him, all his angels: praise ye him, all his hosts. Praise ye him, sun and moon: praise him, all ye stars of light. Praise him, ye heavens of heavens, and ye waters that be above the heavens. Let them praise the name of the Lord: for he commanded, and they were created" (Psalm 148:1-5).

Praise is a celebration of victory. It has already been taken care of over two thousand years ago: our healing, our salvation, our deliverance, or whatever the need, God has made provision for it.

Praise is the way to bring God into our situations. When Paul and Silas began to praise the Lord in the prison, it was not an easy thing to do, but it was a sacrifice of praise. Praise in great trial, great sickness, or in any type of difficulty gets heaven involved with our situation. As in the case of Paul and Silas, the very foundations of the prison began to shake and they were set free all because of praise.

One of the best ways to begin to reprogram the mind to speak positive words is through uplifting songs and poetry. Ephesians 5:19 states, "Speaking to yourselves in psalms and hymns and spiritual songs, singing and making melody in your heart to the Lord."

The truth is that God is great! That is an undisputed fact, but when you speak this fact to your inner self, you are confirming to your mind and spirit that it is true. Great hymns that magnify the Lord, which are sung inside the heart, will begin to bring a magnification of God's power into your life. As you speak it inside of you, then the lips utter what you have spoken to yourself, and then heaven begins to smile at the confirmation of your soul.

We are told in Psalm 92:1, "It is a good thing to give thanks unto the LORD, and to sing praises unto thy name, O most High." To give praise is also the will of God as the following verses indicate:

> *In every thing give thanks: for this is the will of God in Christ Jesus concerning you.*
> —I THESSALONIANS 5:18

> *Giving thanks always for all things unto God.*
> —EPHESIANS 5:20

Train Yourself to Speak Positive

But I will hope continually, and will yet praise thee more and more.

—Psalm 71:14

God inhabits the praises of His people (Psalm 22:3); therefore, if people want to have God close to them, they must learn the art of praising Him.

"Let every thing that hath breath praise the Lord. Praise ye the Lord" (Psalm 150:6).

People like to be around those who are *praisers*. It just makes life so much easier to be with a good-natured person than a constant dripping of criticism and contention.

Contentious people stir up an evil fire of discontent and unpleasant feelings as referred to in Proverbs 26:21: "As coals are to burning coals, and wood to fire; so is a contentious man to kindle strife."

It is so easy to tear down, gripe and complain—any foolish person can do this. It takes someone with guts to buck the tide of negative talk and become the one who lifts people around them.

It is good to hear someone say, "Blessed be the Lord, who daily loadeth us with benefits, even the God of our salvation. Selah" (Psalm 68:19).

Not only is it good to be a lifter and to praise God, but also it is good to praise His Word. "In God will I praise his word: in the Lord will I praise his word" (Psalm 56:10).

When we speak of His Word in tones of reverence we are actually giving Him praise. To take the time to talk about what He says is acknowledgment of His supremacy. This is to praise Him.

5. CHOOSE GOOD FRIENDS.

> *If you would have some worthwhile plans*
> *You've got to watch your can't's and can's;*
> *You can't aim low and then rise high;*
> *You can't succeed if you don't try;*
> *You can't go wrong and come out right;*
> *You can't love sin and walk in light;*
> *You can't choose friends of low degree*
> *And expect to soar and see and be.*
> *You can't throw time and means away;*
> *And live sublime from day to day.*

As shown below the Scriptures give advice to stay away from foolish people. Choosing friends is of utmost importance because friends affect a person's heart and soul. What they are will seep into your spirit. Conversations that are held influence and take effect. It is valuable to make friends with wise people, for they help make the listener wise.

- *He that walketh with wise men shall be wise: but a companion of fools shall be destroyed.*
  —PROVERBS 13:20

- *Go from the presence of a foolish man, when thou perceivest not in him the lips of knowledge.*
  —PROVERBS 14:7

- *Make no friendship with an angry man; and with a furious man thou shalt not go: lest thou learn his ways, and get a snare to thy soul.*

   —Proverbs 22:24-25

People's friends rub off on them; therefore, friendships formed are very important. A saying often quoted when we were growing up was, "If you trot with the skunk you will carry the smell." Our parents were always concerned about who our friends were.

I remember when I was a teenager a good-looking young man asked me out for a date and I told him he had to go ask my father if I could go. I remember seeing him and my dad talking on the front steps of the church for quite a long time. When he came to the car, he was mad and threw the car into gear and sped off down the road. He did not say anything for a while, so I said, "What's wrong?"

He angrily said, "Your dad thinks you are too good to go out with me." I remember that was the last date I had with him. It was a chilly atmosphere in the car and we sat far apart from each other. When he took me home he did not get out of the car but just let me out to walk alone to the door. Then he spun off speedily down the road out of my life.

My dad knew the pitfalls of having the wrong friends and later I found out he told the young man that God had His hand on my life and that he only wanted me to date men who were spiritually minded. In other words he thought the young man was too carnal to date his daughter. My dad may not have been wise and tactful, but he was a parent who cared, and probably kept my feet going in the right direction, because the young man was very handsome and I did like him.

Choosing friends is to choose direction, for in forming alliances with people, spirits are melted together, ideas shared, and characters molded.

President George Washington once said, "Associate yourself with men of good quality if you esteem your own reputation; for 'tis better to be alone than in bad company."

BUILDING YOUR HOUSE WITH WORDS

Jesus said that we build a house with His words. "Whosoever cometh to me, and heareth my sayings, and doeth them, I will shew you to whom he is like: He is like a man which built an house, and digged deep, and laid the foundation on a rock: and when the flood arose, the stream beat vehemently upon that house, and could not shake it: for it was founded upon a rock" (Luke 6:47-48).

Jesus also said that the person's house would fall who does not keep His sayings. "But he that heareth, and doeth not, is like a man that without a foundation built an house upon the earth; against which the stream did beat vehemently, and immediately it fell; and the ruin of that house was great" (Luke 6:49).

Some people build spiritual houses that are smaller than what God intended them to be, simply because of their thoughts and speech.

> Some build spiritual shacks on a foundation intended for a skyscraper.
>
> —Dr. H. Henderson[39]

Builders must have blueprints in building a house. Without a blueprint, the structure would be a mess. Every individual needs to have a blueprint that he or she follows in building a house of words.

A plan must be thought about of how to accomplish the task of producing positive words. Anything that is important always has plans attached to it, or something worth keeping a record.

A good plan is to have a journal and checklist of what needs to be done. As each point is accomplished for the day, then put a check mark by it. On another page keep track of good experiences that resulted from positive speaking or bad experiences from negative speech. This helps you see what is happening from day to day. It also helps in developing the pattern for your life.

So keep track of the five things that shape your life and speech: prayer, the Word, friends, God, and the praise habit, which is all about attitude. Examine what areas you are weak in and in what you are strong. Bolster the weak areas and continually work at improving anything that needs to be improved.

"Think"

If you think you are beaten, you are;
If you think you dare not, you don't.
If you'd like to win, but think you can't,
It's almost certain you won't.

If you think you'll lose, you're lost,
For out in the world we find
Success begins with a fellow's will;
It's all in the state of the mind.

If you think you're outclassed, you are;
You've got to think high to rise.
You've just got to be sure of yourself
Before you can win the prize.

Life's battles don't always go
To the stronger or faster man,
But sooner or later the man who wins
Is the one who thinks he can.

—Author Unknown[40]

7

SPEAK VICTORY

There was a famous football coach, Knute Rockne, who it was said could "talk the birds out of the magnolias."[41] He was the one who helped to develop the forward pass and make it famous and also brought Notre Dame fame. While he was coach he had a player on his team named George Gipp, who became quite a star player—one of the best. In 1920 George suffered a serious illness from which he did not recover. Before he died he told the coach in a whispering voice, "Sometimes when things are going wrong, when the breaks are beating the boys, tell them to go out and win one for the Gipper."

It was in 1928 and Notre Dame was playing the Army's football team and they were up against it. The first half they scored zero points. At halftime Coach Rockne went into the locker room and gave them a short speech, relating what George Gipp had said, and then challenged them to "Win it for the Gipper." The team went out on the field and won the game. The words spoken so passionately from the coach spurred them on to victory. Through the tongue he had the power to inspire others to win.

SPEAK BEFORE A VICTORY

David spoke victory *before* the victory. In the tent of the king on a rocky mountainside, a young man, unseasoned and untrained, spoke words of victory, while the rest of the army hid behind rocks and trembled with fear in their hearts.

"David said moreover, The LORD that delivered me out of the paw of the lion, and out of the paw of the bear, he will deliver me out of the hand of this Philistine. And Saul said unto David, Go, and the LORD be with thee" (I Samuel 17:37).

David went toward the giant Goliath and again David spoke victory before the battle. "Then said David to the Philistine, Thou comest to me with a sword, and with a spear, and with a shield: but I come to thee in the name of the LORD of hosts, the God of the armies of Israel, whom thou hast defied. This day will the LORD deliver thee into mine hands; and I will smite thee, and take thine head from thee; and I will give the carcases of the host of the Philistines this day unto the fowls of the air, and to the wild beasts of the earth; that all the earth may know that there is a God in Israel" (I Samuel 17:45-46).

Sure enough as he had spoken Goliath fell down dead with one rock thrown from the sling of David, and the Philistines ran like scared rabbits.

David spoke it before it happened. God heard David's voice of faith and belief, and He stood behind him and helped make his word come to pass.

Faith is portrayed by actions but also by words.

Words spoken from the mouth have power as demonstrated in the following scriptures.

Romans 10:8: "The word of faith is nigh thee, even in thy mouth."
Hebrews 11:3: "The worlds were framed by the word of God."
Matthew 8:16: Jesus "cast out the spirits with his word."
I Timothy 4:6: "Nourished up in the words of faith."

Another time at another place a word was spoken that formed a whole new world to a man whose world was falling apart. Naaman, captain of the host of the king of Syria, was a great man but he was a leper.

His wife had a little maid who saw the need and spoke victory into an impossible situation.

"And she said unto her mistress, Would God my lord were with the prophet that is in Samaria! for he would recover him of his leprosy" (II Kings 5:3).

When Naaman heard the word, he went to see the prophet Elisha to receive his healing. The prophet spoke a word and told him to go dip in the muddy Jordan seven times and he would be healed.

Naaman was enraged and refused to dip in the muddy river. "Why couldn't he have chosen a cleaner river," he screamed. His servants seeing the dilemma spoke to him and said that if the prophet would have asked him to do something great he would have done it. "This may not be a great thing, but will bring healing: just wash and be clean," they reasoned.

Naaman was persuaded by their words and went to the river and obeyed. "Then went he down, and dipped himself seven times in Jordan, according to the saying of the man of God: and his flesh came again like unto the flesh of a little child, and he was clean" (II Kings 5:14).

Naaman's healing started with the words spoken by his wife's maid as she said, "He will be healed if he will go to the prophet in my land." It all began with a word of faith spoken before anything had happened.

> *Faith is dead to doubts, dumb to discouragements, blind to impossibilities, knows nothing but success. Faith lifts its hands up through the threatening clouds, lays hold of Him who has all power in heaven and on earth. Faith makes the uplook good, the outlook bright, the inlook favorable, and the future glorious.*
>
> —Dr. V. Raymond Edman[42]

SPEAK VICTORY IN TIMES OF CRISIS

During a lifetime, there are many experiences that come to all, things that are not of our choosing. I remember once while helping to nurse our son during an illness that plagued his body, that I chose to do what this chapter is all about: speak victory!

I was awakened at 3:00 in the morning by the cry of pain coming from his room. We had been fighting this sickness and seemingly losing, but this night a fight came into my spirit that was born of God.

I walked into that room and there in my robe, I stood in the middle of the floor and said with a loud voice these words: "And this is the confidence that we have in him, that, if we ask any thing according to his will, he heareth us: and if we know that he hear us, whatsoever we ask, we know that we have the petitions that we desired of him" (I John 5:14-15).

I said, "God, it is your will to heal as stated in III John 2: 'Beloved, I wish above all things that thou mayest prosper and be in health, even as thy soul prospereth.'"

In the face of the spirit of sickness and death, I fought back with words from the Bible. I refused to believe anything else but what I was speaking. Did God hear what was spoken in the wee hours of the morning, during a crisis in our life?

Oh yes, He heard! That Word began to attack the sickness in the body and instead of death overtaking our son, life began slowly to seep back into his body. Gradually, he began to gain strength as we fought our way to victory.

When sickness comes, speak the Word. "I shall not die, but live, and declare the works of the LORD" (Psalm 118:17). Speak victory even when you do not feel like speaking it.

Jesus said, "Heaven and earth shall pass away, but my words shall not pass away" (Matthew 24:35). It is best to speak words that will never pass away, for they are eternal. You can speak words that will last: this is victory!

SPEAK SALVATION

A certain woman named Lydia, a seller of purple who lived in the city of Thyatira, heard words that changed her life on the bank of a river. "And on the sabbath we went out of the city by a river side, where prayer was wont to be made; and we sat down, and spake unto the women which resorted thither" (Acts 16:13).

Paul and Silas spoke to Lydia the word of the Lord and of salvation and she was baptized at the river. Then she opened her house to them and became a great woman of hospitality to the Christians. "And when she was baptized, and her household, she besought us, saying, If ye have judged me to be faithful to the Lord, come into my house, and abide there. And she constrained us" (Acts 16:15).

Lydia became the first convert in Europe all because of words that were spoken to her down by the river. Spoken words of conviction, power, and light—what a wonder! She received the gospel of Christ because two men chose to speak of salvation that day.

Psalm 107:1-2 says for the redeemed to speak: "O give thanks unto the LORD, for he is good: for his mercy endureth for ever. Let the redeemed of the LORD say so." We are commanded to *say so*.

On the Day of Pentecost when they were all filled with the gift of the Holy Ghost, they "all . . . began to speak with other tongues." From there they went out and spoke everywhere of Jesus and the glorious experience of His Spirit. The redeemed of the Lord was *saying so*.

Witnessing is a means of grace for the soul.
It is to the soul what a draft is to a stove.
Shut the mouth, and the fire dies down;
Keep the mouth open, and the fire burns.

—M. TAYLOR

SPEAK VICTORY IN SPITE OF

Most people have some time or other made the statement, "Oh, I wish I'd never said that, or I wish I'd never done that." With dread and regret they experience agony over mere words and bygone actions.

The way a person speaks can bring joy or regret to their inner self. This is proven in Proverbs 15:23: "A man hath joy by the answer of his mouth: and a word spoken in due season, how good is it!"

All of us have spoken words that cause us to experience trepidation, but we have a choice: try to make it right and then go on, or we can dwell on it and be miserable. Spoken words are gone and can never be retrieved. In spite of our situation, we must not continually berate ourselves, neither should we keep repeating the same mistake.

Learn to speak and act positive no matter what happens to you. If you have done something that is gnawing at your insides, take it to God, work it out with Him, and then go on.

To keep reminding yourself of your mistake and to keep rehashing yesterday's dumb things you said and did are not wise. Wisdom says to learn and become wiser.

Develop the habit of looking on the positive side of things and to speak it. I read about a lady who was having lunch with a friend and she was trying to make her see the positive side of something she viewed as negative. The friend suddenly remarked, "You're beginning to sound like Pollyanna."

The lady said much to her surprise she blurted out, "What's so terrible about Pollyanna, anyway? What's wrong with feeling good about life despite the obstacles in your way? What's wrong with looking at the sun instead of seeing gloom and doom? What's wrong with trying to see good in everything? Nothing is wrong with it," she asserted. "In fact," she added, "why would anyone resist thinking that way?"

People say this kind of attitude is not realistic. This is absurd. Who made the rule that negative is realistic? It is all how a person views things. You can choose to be pessimistic or positive, but remember the Book of all books is very positive. Read it and choose words to say loudly in the face of problems and circumstances.

Romans 8:31 should shut up our doubts, and cause us to develop a victorious spirit in spite of what happens: "What shall we then say to these things? If God be for us, who can be against us?"

Speak Faith Not Doubt

It is easy to speak faith when all is well, but more difficult to speak it when all is wrong, but this is the true test of faith.

It was Habakkuk who said, "Yet I will rejoice in the Lord," when he looked at the vines without fruit, the fields with no yield, the stalls with no herd, and the failed olive crop. He spoke faith in His God even in the midst of failure.

Abraham believed even when the promise of God seemingly failed. He kept building an altar and staggered not at the promises even though they were long in coming.

These men are winners. No matter what the circumstance, where it happens, who is involved in it, or how it happened, if God's Word says something that is in favor of you winning, then believe the promise more than the circumstance!

After being filled with the Holy Spirit, there is a power that works in us, stated in the following three scriptures:

- *Ephesians 3:20*: "Now unto him that is able to do exceeding abundantly above all that we ask or think, according to the power that worketh in us."
- *I Thessalonians 2:13*: "For this cause also thank we God without ceasing, because, when ye received the word of God which ye heard of us, ye received it not as the word of men, but as it is in truth, the word of God, which effectually worketh also in you that believe."
- *Colossians 1:29*: "Whereunto I also labour, striving according to his working, which worketh in me mightily."

There it is: we have a power that works in us. We can cancel the fullness of that power from working by what we speak. This is proven many times in the Scripture. Mark 6 tells the story of how Jesus wanted to do miracles and heal people in His hometown, but they questioned His authority because they did not respect who He was. They *spoke* away what He really wanted to do.

"And he could there do no mighty work, save that he laid his hands upon a few sick folk, and healed them. And he marvelled because of their unbelief" (Mark 6:5-6).

In the Old Testament, God did not force the children of Israel to go into Canaan. They *spoke* their way out of the blessing. God could not work as mightily in their behalf because they refused to believe in His power.

"So we see that they could not enter in because of unbelief" (Hebrews 3:19). How was that unbelief manifested? Through the mouth, for Numbers 13:32 says, "And they brought up an *evil report* of the land which they had searched unto the children of Israel."

Speak faith even when weak. Speak faith even during the hottest trial. Speak faith when your very existence is threatened, for faith is needed most when the dark clouds surround you and the sun is obscured.

Whether faith is shouted aloud in the hardship, or spoken softly because of a weakened body, the voice of faith will be heard and God will respond!

> *Faith is the tongue by which we taste how good the Lord is. A feverish tongue is nevertheless a tongue. And even then we may believe when we are without the smallest portion of comfort; for our faith is founded not upon feelings but upon the promises of God.*
> —GEORGE MUELLER

"I Was Born to Win"

I was born to win!
Though difficulties stand in the way
And darkness hides the light of day
I choose to speak faith, not defeat;
It matters not the fire and the heat.

I was born to win!
Defiant words flung into the night
Reaching upward with all my might.
For nothing can keep me down for long,
I'll just speak victory and sing a song.

I was born to win!
Though other tongues may seek to slay,
Trial and misfortune—come what may,
It doesn't matter the time or place
I will make it by His grace!

For I was born to win!

—Joy L. Haney

8

SPEAK LIKE A WINNER

Negative people seldom win. The tongue is an integral part of the winning process. As words are spoken they become pulsating energy that is loosed into the atmosphere. There is a God who listens to every word we speak. Why not learn to speak the way He desires us to speak? You say, "Does God really listen to every single person?"

Yes, He hears even every idle word. In the book of Malachi, the story is told of how God was listening to the people speak even when they were not aware of it. "Your words have been stout against me, saith the LORD. Yet ye say, What have we spoken so much against thee? Ye have said, It is vain to serve God: and what profit is it that we have kept his ordinance, and that we have walked mournfully before the LORD of hosts?" (Malachi 3:13-14).

While there were those who did not care what God thought, there were some who did care. Their reaction to God's words is reflected in Malachi 3:16: "Then they that feared the LORD spake often one to another: and the LORD hearkened, and heard it, and a book of remembrance was written before him for them that feared the LORD, and that thought upon his name."

Notice they *spoke* reverently about the Lord and *thought* upon his name. What was the result of this combination of *speaking* and *thinking* about the Lord? "And they shall be mine, saith the LORD of hosts, in that day when I make up my jewels; and I will spare them, as a man spareth his own son that serveth him" (Malachi 3:17).

WINNERS EXPECT TO WIN!

"Our God has boundless resources. The only limit is in us. Our asking, our thinking, our praying are too small. Our expectations are too limited," so wrote A. B. Simpson.[43]

Winners have an inner voice that says, "I'm going to win." They expect it. Do or die, whatever comes, they are going to win. For years I have read the following poem, but it hit me, the same applies to God. *Life would have paid*, but it is the same with God. He would do so much more for us if we believed Him for it, and would allow our minds to become *deposit centers* of faith and power words to be programmed into them. The possibilities are limitless if only we expect to win and to go beyond what we have ever done before.

"MY WAGE"
I bargained with Life for a penny,
*   And Life would pay no more,*
However I begged at evening
*   When I counted my scanty store;*
For Life is a just employer,
*   He gives you what you ask,*

But once you have set the wages,
 Why, you must bear the task.

I worked for a menial's hire,
 Only to learn, dismayed,
That any wage I had asked of Life,
 Life would have paid.
—Jessie B. Rittenhouse[44]

We settle for less when we could have more if we would just believe. When Jesus was on earth, He continually told the people to believe as shown in the following scriptures:

- *Mark 9:23*: "Jesus said unto him, If thou canst believe, all things are possible to him that believeth."
- *Mark 5:36*: "Be not afraid, only believe."
- *Matthew 21:22*: "And all things, whatsoever ye shall ask in prayer, believing, ye shall receive."
- *Matthew 9:29*: "According to your faith be it unto you."
- *Mark 11:24*: "Therefore I say unto you, What things soever ye desire, when ye pray, believe that ye receive them, and ye shall have them."
- *Matthew 7:7*: "Ask, and it shall be given you; seek, and ye shall find; knock, and it shall be opened unto you."

We must believe and expect to win even in the worst conditions. We must believe no matter if we cannot see our way clear, for as Augustine said, "Faith is to believe what we do not see, and the reward of this faith is to see what we believe."

Even if we do not know everything, we must still expect to win. Said Thomas Edison, "We do not know one-millionth part of one per cent about anything. We do not know what water is. We don't know what light is. We do not know what electricity is. We do not know what gravity is. We don't know anything about magnetism. We have a lot of hypotheses, but that is all."[45]

Winners may not know everything, but they expect victory. Joshua had his men march around the walls of Jericho thirteen times and did not know what would happen, but he expected the walls to fall down because that is what God spoke.

> *He takes my whispered, silent prayer,*
> *My faith like mustard seed*
> *And makes what once was vague and dim*
> *Reality indeed!*
>
> —CHORSTEN CHRISTENSEN

WINNERS SPEAK GRACIOUS WORDS OF OTHERS

Winners are so on fire with their passion and goals, and their minds are in the creative mode, so much that they do not have time to knock others down or seek to destroy. They are too busy building.

Oh, that everyone would seek to adopt the philosophy of one of our founding fathers:

> "I will speak ill of no man, not even in the matter of truth, but rather excuse the faults I

hear, and, upon proper occasions, speak all the good I know of everybody."

—Benjamin Franklin[46]

Paul gave instructions on what the speech should be and it deals with a gracious tongue. Gracious people do not undermine other people, for they have the spirit of a winner and they want others to win.

Colossians 4:6 admonished us to have salted speech: "Let your speech be alway with grace, seasoned with salt, that ye may know how ye ought to answer every man."

One of the most requested items at a dinner table is the salt. "Please, pass the salt" is heard every day at most tables. Salt makes things taste better and gives it flavor. Our spoken conversation should make things better and be always imparted with grace or kindness.

We should seek to be like our Creator. When God descended in a cloud and came near Moses, He proclaimed: "The Lord, The Lord God, merciful and gracious, longsuffering, and abundant in goodness and truth" (Exodus 34:6).

When God spoke, Moses fell to the ground with his head bowed and worshiped the Lord. A good position for all of us to adopt in life: bowing humbly in His presence.

Oh if only we could seek to be gracious and good like our Lord! He is our example of goodness and righteousness.

Both men and women should seek to speak gracious words. Proverbs 11:16 states: "A gracious women retaineth honour," and Ecclesiastes 10:12 paints a picture of a wise man and a fool: "The words of a wise man's mouth are gracious; but the lips of a fool will swallow up himself."

The lips, the mouth, determine whether a man is a fool or a gracious man. What power in speech!

When Jesus spoke words of compassion and power, Luke 4:22 records the people's reaction to His words: "And all bare him witness, and wondered at the gracious words which proceeded out of his mouth."

He was our great example as written in I Peter 2:21-22: "For even hereunto were ye called: because Christ also suffered for us, leaving us an example, that ye should follow his steps: who did no sin, neither was guile found in his mouth."

To follow in His steps is the greatest adventure of a lifetime. To allow His Spirit to live within us and dominate our thoughts and lips is beyond description. There is nothing like walking with Jesus and listening to His voice and feeling His presence with us all the time!

WINNERS DO NOT COMPLAIN

To complain is to express discontent, or dissatisfaction. Complainers usually whine and go on and on about something that is bothering them. They speak in a plaintive tone, and their woe is heard by anyone who will listen.

The lament or expression of suffering and woe is a broken record in their minds; therefore, they speak it every day. Just like they eat their daily bread, they also partake of their complaining ritual.

> "To know when to keep silent is one of the finest of arts. The atmosphere of life is darkened

> by murmuring and whispering over the non-essentials, the trifles that are inevitably incident to the hurly-burly of the day's routine. Things cannot always go our way. Learn to accept in silence the minor aggravations. Cultivate the gift of quietude and consume your own smoke with an extra draught of hard work so that those about you may not be annoyed with the dust and soot of your complaints."
>
> —WILLIAM OSLER, M.D.[47]

There is nothing more disheartening than being in the presence of someone with a constant drip of complaints. Nothing is ever right; they always have a problem. This continual verbiage is draining on the listener and on the speaker also.

People choose whether or not to complain. Some things in life are such that it would be easy to complain because of the justification of the problem, but there are other things that come and go about which all of us will choose to complain with heatedness or to do something else with our complaint.

How true this is. There have been times in my life when I felt steamed up about a situation. Instead of complaining and bellyaching I would begin to clean the house or do a chore that required physical exercise. If it were in the kitchen the pots may have banged a little louder, the cabinet doors shut a little harder, but as I worked, the steam worked its way out of me. The only thing that got hurt would have been maybe a kick to the object lying on the floor that should not have been there, or the pot that was banged harder than needed to be, but at least the feelings of others were not hurt.

Phillips Brooks once said, "Life is too short to nurse one's misery. Hurry across the lowlands, that you may spend more time on the mountaintops."

There is a phrase in Isaiah 30:15 that fits here: "In quietness and in confidence shall be your strength." It was Martin Luther who said, "Suffer and be still and tell no man thy sorrow; trust in God—His help will not fail thee." To tell a friend or to have someone pray is fine, but to have a continual complaint is not good.

> *Talk much of one's sorrow makes one weak, but to tell one's sorrow to Him Who heareth in secret, makes one strong and calm.*
>
> —THOLUCK

Complainers are rarely happy people. They live in misery and are often vexed with problems. Complaining becomes a way of life, a habit that is like a prison to the personality. The person is enclosed behind bars because they keep the wretchedness inside them and tell everyone about it. What they need to do is take it to the Lord in prayer and stay at His feet until the burden is unloaded completely, and until a song comes into their spirit as the following poem asks:

The little sharp vexations
And the briars that catch and fret,
Why not take all to the Helper
Who has never failed us yet?

Tell Him about the heartache,
And tell Him the longings, too;
Tell Him the baffled purpose
When we scarce know what to do
Then, leaving all our weakness
With the One divinely strong,
Forget that we bore the burden,
And carry away the song.

—MARGARET SANGSTER

A WINNER'S SPEECH REFLECTS PASSION

Winners exude passion. Sam Walton, the developer of Wal-Mart in America, shared ten rules on building a business. The following is rule number one: "COMMIT to your business. Believe in it more than anybody else. I think I overcame every single one of my personal shortcomings by the sheer passion I brought to my work. I don't know if you're born with this kind of passion, or if you can learn it. But I do know you need it. If you love your work, you'll be out there every day trying to do the best you possibly can, and pretty soon everybody around will catch the passion from you—like a fever."[48]

It is good to have passion to win in life. People should seek to attain and become, but even greater than life itself is the attainment of entering into heaven. This should be the goal of every person.

Saul who persecuted the church before his dramatic introduction to Christ was a very passionate man for the cause for which he was fighting. This same spirit characterized his zeal for the work of Christ's kingdom after having been filled with His Spirit.

His speech was so convincing concerning the gospel of Jesus Christ, that when he was in prison, they had to change the guards every four hours because he was converting them.

No matter what situation he found himself in, he always came out a winner. Romans 8:35 lists some of the things that tried to separate him from his love and passion: "Who shall separate us from the love of Christ? shall tribulation, or distress, or persecution, or famine, or nakedness, or peril, or sword?" He summed it up like this: "Nay, in all these things we are more than conquerors through him that loved us. For I am persuaded, that neither death, nor life, nor angels, nor principalities, nor powers, nor things present, nor things to come, nor height, nor depth, nor any other creature, shall be able to separate us from the love of God, which is in Christ Jesus our Lord" (Romans 8:37-39).

What an attitude! Nothing could keep him down. He just kept coming back no matter what came his way. You can put a winner in a vise and he will find a way to squeeze out of it. Paul was such a man.

Paul said, "I have fought!" He fought for the things he believed in and was passionate in his zeal for the Lord, but his passion did not take away his adversaries. They were there all the time, but neither did they dim his passion.

I Corinthians 16:9 bears this out: "For a great door and effectual is opened unto me, and there are many adversaries." This was the story of his life. He was stoned, beaten, lied about, put in prison, among other things, but Paul's passion never waned.

Did he win? II Timothy 4:8 says he did: "Henceforth there is laid up for me a crown of righteousness, which the Lord, the righteous judge, shall give me at that day."

His passion for the cause kept him in the most excruciating circumstances and he was able to say like a winner: "I have fought a good fight, I have finished my course, I have kept the faith" (II Timothy 4:7).

WINNERS HAVE HAPPY TONGUES

"Principal Rainy, of whom a child once remarked that she believed he went to heaven every night because he was so happy every day, once used a fine metaphor about a Christian's joy. 'Joy,' he said, 'is the flag which is flown from the castle of the heart when the King is in residence there.'"[49]

Psalm 126:2 describes the happy tongue: "Then was our mouth filled with laughter, and our tongue with singing: then said they among the heathen, The LORD hath done great things for them."

The Lord does great things for his children every day. He gives health, strength, life, water to drink and use, joy, peace, and answers prayers time and time again; He is always there for His people. We should sing of His greatness no matter what happens because sooner or later He will work everything out according to His plan.

We are commanded to sing a new song in Psalm 98:1: "O sing unto the LORD a new song; for he hath done marvellous things: his right hand, and his holy arm, hath gotten him the victory."

Further instructions for a winner are given in Psalm 100:1-5:

Verse 1: "Make a joyful noise unto the LORD, all ye lands."

Verse 2: "Serve the LORD with gladness: come before his presence with singing."

Verse 3: "Know ye that the LORD he is God: it is he that hath made us, and not we ourselves; we are his people, and the sheep of his pasture."

Verse 4: "Enter into his gates with thanksgiving, and into his courts with praise: be thankful unto him, and bless his name."

Verse 5: "For the LORD is good; his mercy is everlasting; and his truth endureth to all generations."

Take time to sing of His mercy, of His goodness, of His everlasting love, for He alone is great and greatly to be praised.

A favorite song to sing is as follows:

> *Sing unto the Lord a new song,*
> *Sing unto the Lord all the earth.*
> *Sing unto the Lord a new song.*
> *Sing unto the Lord all the earth.*
> *For God is great! And greatly to be praised!*
> *God is great! And greatly to be praised!*

Psalm 149:5 declares: "Let the saints be joyful in glory: let them sing aloud upon their beds." Amos R. Wells says, "Yes, let all Christians sing, even on beds of pain. Let all Christians sing, evensongs in the night, evensongs in prison, like Paul and Silas. Few lives are so songful as they might be and should be. Most lives are groanful. Most lives are full of complaint, meditated if not uttered aloud."

"Accept My Full Heart's Thanks"

Your words came just when needed.
Like a breeze,
Blowing and bringing from the wide salt sea
Some cooling spray, to meadow scorched with heat
And choked with dust and clouds of sifted sand
That hateful whirlwind, envious of its bloom,
Had tossed upon it. But the cool sea breeze
Came laden with the odors of the sea
And damp with spray, that laid the dust and sand
And brought new life and strength to blade and bloom
So words of thine came over miles to me,
Fresh from the mighty sea, a true friend's heart,
And brought me hope, and strength, and swept away
The dusty webs that human spiders spun
Across my path. Friend—and the word means much—
So few there are who reach like thee, a hand
Up over all the barking curs of spite
And give the clasp, when most its need is felt,
Friend, newly found, accept my full heart's thanks.

—Ella Wheeler Wilcox[50]

9
SPEAK A BLESSING

Speak a blessing if you want a blessing. Ecclesiastes 11:1 proves that whatever is sent out will come back: "Cast thy bread upon the waters: for thou shalt find it after many days."

This principle is substantiated in Luke 6:37-38: "Judge not, and ye shall not be judged: condemn not, and ye shall not be condemned: forgive, and ye shall be forgiven: give, and it shall be given unto you; good measure, pressed down, and shaken together, and running over, shall men give into your bosom. For with the same measure that ye mete withal it shall be measured to you again."

Whatever is given out from you will be multiplied back to you, so why not hand out blessings? What is it you want? That is what you must give in order to receive.

The following three categories of blessings will be discussed in this chapter:
- Bless God.
- Bless people.
- Bless yourself.

BLESS GOD

In the Old Testament the story is told that during the time Ezra brought all the people together to read the law, there was great respect and reverence for God. They stood for hours and listened to the law being read.

Then several of the Levites with great emotion said: "Stand up and bless the LORD your God for ever and ever: and blessed be thy glorious name, which is exalted above all blessing and praise. Thou, even thou, art LORD alone; thou hast made heaven, the heaven of heavens, with all their host, the earth, and all things that are therein, the seas, and all that is therein, and thou preservest them all; and the host of heaven worshippeth thee" (Nehemiah 9:5b-6).

The psalmist David declared in Psalm 34:1, "I will bless the LORD at all times: his praise shall continually be in my mouth."

To bless the Lord at all times is the best thing a person can do for himself, for others, and for his God.

It should be our commandment: "O bless our God, ye people, and make the voice of his praise to be heard" (Psalm 66:8).

The New Testament continues with this theme of praising and blessing the Lord: "Let us offer the sacrifice of praise to God continually, that is, the fruit of our lips giving thanks to his name" (Hebrews 13:15).

The Amplified Version of this verse states, "Through Him, therefore, let us constantly and at all times offer up to God a sacrifice of praise, which is the fruit of lips that thankfully acknowledge and confess and glorify His name."

Our lips are to confess or speak of His name and to praise Him at all times. It is when we are in times of difficulty that it becomes a sacrifice. A sacrifice is anything that is given up for something better. That something better is God's blessing and approval, for God is interested in our reactions in the fiery furnaces of life. We are to bless the Lord no matter what happens to us, especially in the midnights of our life.

Jesus spoke in Matthew 7:20: "Wherefore by their fruits ye shall know them." If what our lips speak is called fruit, then where does the fruit come from? Fruit is usually grown on a tree. Trees are usually grown together in what are called orchards. From the orchards fruit is shipped to factories, stores and distribution centers. In the orchard there can be fruit that is touched with the gold of the sun, so ripe and beautiful that it makes people ooh and aah, or the fruit can be dried up, shriveled and bitter tasting. It depends on the proper amount of water, sun and cultivation that the orchard received.

Each of us grows an orchard inside of us that produces fruit. The mouth is the gate to the orchard and the *fruit of the lips* is the shipping point. It is important to let the Sun of Righteousness shine inside, and the water of the Spirit flow through the inner person and to make the cultivation of the Word a daily thing. Then the fruit of the lips will be beautiful and blessed.

Reinforced over and over is the concept of blessing the Lord. The following scriptures demonstrate this:

Psalm 16:7a: "I will bless the LORD, who hath given me counsel."

Psalm 63:3-4: "Because thy lovingkindness is better than life, my lips shall praise thee. Thus will I bless thee while I live: I will lift up my hands in thy name."

Psalm 145:1-5, 11, 21:

Verse 1: "I will extol thee, my God, O king; and I will bless thy name for ever and ever."

Verse 2: "Every day will I bless thee; and I will praise thy name for ever and ever."

Verse 3: "Great is the LORD, and greatly to be praised; and his greatness is unsearchable."

Verse 4: "One generation shall praise thy works to another, and shall declare thy mighty acts."

Verse 5: "I will speak of the glorious honour of thy majesty, and of thy wondrous works."

Verse 11: "They shall speak of the glory of thy kingdom, and talk of thy power."

Verse 21: "My mouth shall speak the praise of the LORD: and let all flesh bless his holy name for ever and ever."

> "To exist is to bless; life is happiness. In this sublime pause of things all dissonances have disappeared. It is as though creation were but one vast symphony, glorifying the God of goodness with an inexhaustible wealth of praise and harmony. We question no longer whether it is so or not. We have ourselves become notes in the great concert; and the soul breaks the silence of ecstasy only to vibrate in unison with the eternal joy."
>
> —HENRY FREDERIC AMIEL[51]

BLESS PEOPLE

The principle of blessing has been from the beginning of time. Genesis records how Jacob blessed his twelve sons: "All these are the twelve tribes of Israel: and this is it that their father spake unto them, and blessed them; every one according to his blessing he blessed them" (Genesis 49:28).

The subject of blessing is found in Peter's writings. He talked about the tongue being the key to life and blessing as shown in the following passage:

I Peter 3:8-12:
Verse 8: "Finally, be ye all of one mind, having compassion one of another, love as brethren, be pitiful, be courteous:"
Verse 9: "Not rendering evil for evil, or railing for railing: but contrariwise blessing; knowing that ye are thereunto called, that ye should inherit a blessing."
Verse 10: "For he that will love life, and see good days, let him refrain his tongue from evil, and his lips that they speak no guile:"
Verse 11: "Let him eschew evil, and do good; let him seek peace, and ensue it."
Verse 12: "For the eyes of the Lord are over the righteous, and his ears are open unto their prayers: but the face of the Lord is against them that do evil."

Evil in this passage has to do with what a person speaks. He admonishes us to be in *one mind*, to love one another and to be courteous, not to speak evil but blessing instead. Why? Because the blessing is our inheritance if we speak right! The Lord promises if we want to love life and see good days, then we must not speak evil, but hate evil, do good, and seek peace.

This is powerful! We ourselves are blessed by what we speak of others and to others. Just as important it is to mean what we say. David penned this phrase in Psalm 62:4, "They bless with their mouth, but they curse inwardly." This is an atrocious thing which God will punish in His time.

The principle in the Bible is to bless those who curse you. This is opposite of what we are told today, but the blessings of the Lord are upon them who obey the Word of God. Peter instructed us to give blessing for evil: "Not rendering evil for evil, but blessing." This concept is found in the following scriptures:

Matthew 5:44: "But I say unto you, Love your enemies, bless them that curse you, do good to them that hate you, and pray for them which despitefully use you, and persecute you."

Romans 12:14: "Bless them which persecute you: bless, and curse not."

I Corinthians 4:12: "And labour, working with our own hands: being reviled, we bless; being persecuted, we suffer it."

It should become the habit of Christians to say "God bless you," and mean it, as was so beautifully penned in the following poem:

"God Bless You"
I seek in prayerful words, dear friend,
My heart's true wish to send you,

That you may know that, far or near,
  My loving thoughts attend you.

I cannot find a truer word,
  Nor better to address you;
Nor song, nor poem have I heard
  Is sweeter than God bless you!

God bless you! So I've wished you all
  Of brightness life possesses;
For can there any joy at all
  Be yours unless God blesses?

God bless you! So I breathe a charm
  Lest grief's dark night oppress you,
For how can sorrow bring you harm
  If 'tis God's way to bless you?

And so, "through all thy days
  May shadows touch thee never"
But this alone—God bless thee—
  Then art thou safe forever.

—Author Unknown[52]

As we bless others, we are blessing ourselves. We would do well to keep the blessings coming, for life without them can be a long, hard road, but the blessings of the Lord bring sunshine, hope, and healing to parched souls in need of His blessings.

When I was host of the radio weekly prayer meeting that was aired to thousands of people, often I would read the blessing in Numbers 6:24-26, which I give to you now:

> *The LORD bless thee, and keep thee: The LORD make his face shine upon thee, and be gracious unto thee: The LORD lift up his countenance upon thee, and give thee peace.*

A faithful man shall abound with blessings.
—PROVERBS 28:20

Blessings are upon the head of the just.
—PROVERBS 10:6

BLESS YOURSELF

Blessings are ours. Psalm 3:8 declares: "Salvation belongeth unto the LORD: thy blessing is upon thy people. Selah."

The story of Caleb was related in the first chapter. At age eighty he asked for a mountain. He reminded Joshua of the promise of the Lord forty years earlier, and spoke "Give me this mountain." Caleb was asking for a blessing.

It is interesting to note that the daughter of Caleb had the same spirit as her father. The story is told in Joshua 15:18-19: "And it came to pass, as she [Achsah] came unto him, that she moved him to ask of her father a field: and she lighted off her ass; and Caleb said unto her, What wouldest thou? Who answered, Give me a blessing; for thou hast given me a south land; give me also springs of water. And he gave her the upper springs, and the nether springs."

Achsah asked for a blessing and she received it. "Give me the springs of water" is what she wanted. Land without water is not as valuable, so she wanted not only the land, but also the water.

We as God's children have the same right to ask blessings of our heavenly Father. It is our inheritance. "The blessing of the LORD, it maketh rich, and he addeth no sorrow with it" (Proverbs 10:22).

"Give me Your blessings, Lord," should be our cry. It is not wrong to want the Lord to bless us with health, strength, joy, happiness, sustenance, and so many things that are our inheritance.

It was Jabez who prayed the prayer: "Bless me Lord, indeed." There is nothing wrong with asking for the blessing of the Lord upon you.

As His children we can speak the things God has promised us. They are His blessings, so why not speak them and expect them? So many things to say, why not begin to speak what is ours?

- We should speak *health*.

Proverbs 12:18: "The tongue of the wise is *health*." What we speak brings us health. Our hope in Him brings health to our inner being as the psalmist declares: "Hope in God: for I shall yet praise him, who is the health of my countenance" (Psalm 43:5).

Praise given to God brings health to the giver. Our words bring sweetness to our soul and health to the part of the body that builds good blood: "Pleasant words are as an honeycomb, sweet to the soul, and health to the bones" (Proverbs 16:24).

"My soul shall be satisfied as with marrow and fatness; and my mouth shall praise thee with joyful lips: . . . because thou hast been my help" (Psalm 63:5 & 7a).

It pleases God, and his pleasure brings health as shown in Psalm 69:30-32: "I will praise the name of God with a song, and will magnify him with thanksgiving. This also shall please the LORD better than an ox or bullock that hath horns and hoofs. The humble shall see this, and be glad: and your heart shall live that seek God."

> *Begin to confess, "I feel terrific! Thank you, God, for Your healing. Health is in my body. I am healed in Jesus' name!" As you speak it, your body will respond.*

- We can speak *freedom*.

Proverbs 12:6: "The mouth of the upright shall deliver them." As we confess Christ and are filled with His Spirit, we receive the blessing of salvation and the freedom from sin. Paul spoke of this blessing in Romans 4:7-8: "Blessed are they whose iniquities are forgiven, and whose sins are covered. Blessed is the man to whom the Lord will not impute sin."

> *Jesus was sent to bless us with deliverance. Confess this scripture: "Unto you first God, having raised up his Son Jesus, sent him to bless you, in turning away every one of you from his iniquities."*

- We can speak *increase*.

Increase and blessing come from what we *say* and what we *think*! The following scriptures prove this:

Proverbs 18:20: "A man's belly shall be satisfied with the fruit of his mouth; and with the increase of his lips shall he be filled."

Proverbs 13:2: "A man shall eat good by the fruit of his mouth."

Psalm 1:1-3: "Blessed is the man that walketh not in the counsel of the ungodly, nor standeth in the way of sinners, nor sitteth in the seat of the scornful. But his delight is in the law of the LORD; and in his law doth he meditate day and night. And he shall be like a tree planted by the rivers of water, that bringeth forth his fruit in his season; his leaf also shall not wither; and whatsoever he doeth shall prosper."

Psalm 115:13-14: "He will bless them that fear the LORD, both small and great. The LORD shall increase you more and more, you and your children."

> *It is a fact: God will bless us! "God shall bless us; and all the ends of the earth shall fear him."*
> —PSALM 67:7

- We should speak *good* things.

"Let no corrupt communication proceed out of your mouth, but that which is good to the use of edifying, that it may minister grace unto the hearers" (Ephesians 4:29).

The best way to speak good things is to bless the Lord and his people. When this happens wealth and riches will come as spoken of in Psalm 112:1-3: "Praise ye the LORD. Blessed is the man that feareth the LORD, that delighteth greatly in his commandments. His seed shall be mighty upon earth: the generation of the upright shall be blessed. Wealth and riches shall be in his house: and his righteousness endureth for ever."

> *Pray this prayer: "My times are in thy hand: deliver me from the hand of mine enemies, and from them that persecute me. Make thy face to shine upon thy servant: save them for thy mercies' sake."*
> —PSALM 31:15-16

WORDS SPOKEN CAN ALSO BRING A CURSE!

The opposite of speaking a blessing is to speak a curse. People can actually make bad things happen by what they say. This is proven over and over in the Scripture.

One of these incidents is recorded in the Book of Numbers. Moses had sent twelve spies to go into Canaan to see what the lay of the land looked like and how they could conquer the city. When the twelve men returned to Moses after exploring the land, two of them had a positive report and ten of them a negative report. Caleb and Joshua said, "Let us go up at once, and possess it; for we are well able to overcome it" (Numbers 13:30).

The ten negative men said, "We be not able to go up against the people; for they are stronger than we" (Numbers 13:31). The Bible called this an *evil* report.

The congregation of people began to murmur against Moses and accuse him of bringing them into the wilderness to die. They even said, "Would God that we had died in the land of Egypt! or would God we had died in this wilderness!" (Numbers 14:2). This made God angry and He wanted to kill them, but Moses pled with God, reminding Him of His long-suffering and great mercy, so God relented and the people lived.

Notice what God told Moses: "How long shall I bear with this evil congregation, which murmur against me? I have heard the murmurings of the children of Israel, which they murmur against me. Say unto them, As truly as I live, saith the Lord, as ye have spoken in mine ears, so will I do to you" (Numbers 14:27-28).

This is powerful! The people were not speaking to God; they were speaking to Moses, but all the while God was listening. His ears heard every word they had spoken. They were bringing a curse upon themselves by what they were speaking to Moses and to one another. God said, "As ye have spoken in mine ears, so will I do to you."

What you speak is what you get! They *spoke* that they wanted to die in the wilderness, so that is what they got. "Doubtless ye shall not come into the land, concerning which I sware to make you dwell therein, save Caleb the son of Jephunneh, and Joshua the son of Nun. But your little ones, which ye said should be a prey, them will I bring in, and they shall know the land which ye have despised. But as for you, your carcases, they shall fall in this wilderness. . . . I the Lord have said, I will surely do it unto all this evil congregation, that are gathered together against me: in this wilderness they shall be consumed, and there they shall die" (Numbers 14:30-32; 35).

The strange thing about all this is that they *spoke* it to Moses, but God said they spoke it to Him. Whatever you speak, you are really speaking to God, because He is listening and records every word that is spoken. "But I say unto you, That every idle word that men shall speak, they shall give account thereof in the day of judgment"

(Matthew 12:36). This is a warning! Be careful of the words you SPEAK!

Another incident in the lives of the children of Israel occurred when they journeyed from mount Hor by the way of the Red Sea towards the land of Edom. The soul of the people was much discouraged because of the way. "And the people spake against God, and against Moses, Wherefore have ye brought us up out of Egypt to die in the wilderness? for there is no bread, neither is there any water; and our soul loatheth this light bread" (Numbers 21:5).

The words they spoke were what angered the Lord, so He sent fiery serpents among them and many people died. Because of the pain, agony and death that the serpents incurred, the people went to Moses and asked him to intervene in their behalf.

This was their plea: "We have sinned, for we have spoken against the LORD, and against thee; pray unto the LORD, that he take away the serpents from us. And Moses prayed for the people. And the LORD said unto Moses, Make thee a fiery serpent, and set it upon a pole: and it shall come to pass, that every one that is bitten, when he looketh upon it, shall live" (Numbers 21:7-8).

The people spoke a curse upon themselves by what was uttered out of their mouth. They spoke about death and that is what God sent them.

Another incident occurred involving the family of Moses. Moses' sister Miriam and brother Aaron got together and spoke against Moses concerning the woman he married. "And they said, Hath the LORD indeed spoken only by Moses? hath he not spoken also by us? And the LORD heard it" (Numbers 12:2).

They were speaking among themselves, but God heard what they said. He spoke to Moses and told him to have the three of them come together in the tabernacle of the congregation. So they went and God came down in a pillar of the cloud and spoke. "And he said, Hear now my words: If there be a prophet among you, I the LORD will make myself known unto him in a vision, and will speak unto him in a dream. My servant Moses is not so, who is faithful in all mine house. With him will I speak mouth to mouth, even apparently, and not in dark speeches; and the similitude of the LORD shall he behold: wherefore then were ye not afraid to speak against my servant Moses?" (Numbers 12:6-8).

The anger of the Lord breathed hot upon them and He departed, but when He left, Miriam became leprous, white as snow. This resulted in Miriam being shut out from the camp. Moses, being the meek man that he was, prayed to God for his sister and God had mercy upon Miriam. After seven days she was healed and brought back into the camp.

Incidents such as this cause a conscientious person to pray fervently the prayer, "Let the words of my mouth, and the meditation of my heart, be acceptable in thy sight, O LORD, my strength, and my redeemer" (Psalm 19:14).

There it is again, the *words* of my mouth and the *thoughts* of my heart: words and thoughts. This is what a person really is.

CHOOSE TO SPEAK A BLESSING

We need to get positive with God and do what He says to do. Moses, in speaking to the people, gave them a choice: "Behold, I set before you this day a blessing and a curse; A blessing, if you obey the commandments of the LORD your God, which I command you this day: And a curse, if ye will not obey the commandments of the LORD your God" (Deuteronomy 11:26-28a).

This same challenge or choice is repeated in Deuteronomy 30:19: "I have set before you life and death, blessing and cursing: therefore choose life, that both thou and thy seed may live."

The blessing or curse had to do with *words*: words that were spoken by God. This whole book is about words. Each of us must choose what we do with His words. Obey them and live, ignore them and die. We can have abundant life in Christ or we can live a miserable life, slowly dying, just existing. It is a choice everyone must make, but it involves what we will do with the words God spoke, and the words we will speak.

Everyone makes choices every day. We choose what we do with our life. We choose what words we will speak. We choose friends, we choose what we allow in our minds, we choose to do right or wrong. The following story depicts the end of two men who each made different choices:

"When David Livingstone's body was brought back from Africa to England, great throngs along the streets watched the funeral procession. An elderly man in the crowd burst into sobs. Lamented he, 'I knew Livingstone when I was a young man. We went together. We were friends. When he told me of God's call to him to go to Africa, I ridiculed him. I was ambitious. I chose a life of self-ease. I cared only for my own selfish interests. Now, with a misspent life behind me, I acknowledge that Livingstone made a wise choice when he answered and obeyed God's call. I put the emphasis on the wrong world!'"[53]

The question is what will be your choice today? After reading a whole book about the power of speaking positive, the choice is still yours. What will you do with knowledge? What is important to you? What will your speech emphasize? Do you care enough to change if you have had a problem in the past? Is the Word of God more powerful to you than your own habitual way of speaking? Through the Word there has been light shed on a very important subject. What will you do with it?

I believe that you will join the Joshua and Calebs, the Abraham Lincolns, the Hannahs, the Winston Churchills, David and Daniel, and all the other figures down through history who have made the choice to bless God, bless themselves and bless others. I believe you will make the right choice today.

Epilogue

Paganini, the great violinist, came out before his audience one day and made the discovery just as they ended their applause that there was something wrong with his violin. He looked at it a second and then saw that it was not his famous and valuable one.

He felt paralyzed for a moment, then turned to his audience and told them there had been some mistake and he did not have his own violin. He stepped back behind the curtain thinking that it was still where he had left it, but discovered that someone had stolen his and left that old secondhand one in its place. He remained back of the curtain a moment, then came out before his audience and said: "Ladies and gentlemen: I will show you that the music is not in the instrument, but in the soul." And he played as he had never played before; and out of that secondhand instrument the music poured forth until the audience was enraptured with enthusiasm and the applause almost lifted the ceiling of the building, because the man had revealed to them that music was not in the machine, but in his own soul.

—Story Told by Charles Francis Richardson

Likewise, what is in the soul, heart and mind will be revealed through the mouth. We will all make music today, for our voices transmit intricate tones of rhythm and vibration of words that resonate from sound boxes within.

A voice is a sound produced by vertebrates by means of lungs and the larynx, whereas musical sounds are produced by the vocal folds and resonated by the cavities of head and throat.

The voice has been likened to a fine instrument, which has the ability to make different sounds and with varied pitches. To be voiceless is to be void of sound.

The gift given to us by our Creator of being able to speak is a wonder, and how often we abuse the privilege of being able to speak. May this book inspire you to make a study of learning to speak positive and in a way that is pleasing unto God, for He listens to every word that is spoken and is keeping record of them all.

When we understand that God is recording each word that is uttered then it makes us much more aware of the sound that comes forth from our instrument.

Speak well today! Study His Word, which will give you the best education that anyone could want with which to fill the mind. It will help prepare you for the flight from this world to the next one. For soon the day will come.

"For the Lord himself shall descend from heaven with a shout, with the voice of the archangel, and with the trump of God: and the dead in Christ shall rise first: then we which are alive and remain shall be caught up together with them in the clouds, to meet the Lord in the air: and so shall we ever be with the Lord" (I Thessalonians 4:16-17).

We will meet our words in heaven, the ones that have not been blotted out through repentance, for Jesus spoke in Matthew 12:36: "But I say unto you, That every idle word that men shall speak, they shall give account thereof in the day of judgment."

This is why it is so important to pray the following prayer:

Epilogue

> *"Let the words of my mouth, and the meditation of my heart, be acceptable in thy sight, O LORD, my strength, and my redeemer."*
>
> —Psalm 19:14

Notes

[1] Cho, Dr. Paul Yonggi, *The Fourth Dimension*, (Logos International, Plainfield, NJ: 1979), pp. 67-68.

[2] Cowman, Mrs. Charles E., *Streams in the Desert, Vol. Two*, (Zondervan Publishing House, Grand Rapids, MI: 1966), October 23.

[3] Tan, Paul Lee, ThD., *Encyclopedia of 7,700 Illustrations*, (Assurance Publishers, Rockville, Maryland: 1988), #3133.

[4] Howell, Clinton T., edited by, *Lines to Live By*, (Thomas Nelson, Inc., New York, NY: 1972), p. 32.

[5] Ibid., p. 120.

[6] Tan, #1975.

[7] Alexander, A. L., compiled by, *Poems that Touch the Heart*, (Doubleday, New York, NY: 1941), p. 59.

[8] Johnson, Joseph S., compiled by, *A Field of Diamonds*, (Broadman Press, Nashville, TN: 1974), p. 116.

[9] Howell, p. 18.

[10] Carson, Clayborne & Kris Shepard, edited by, *A Call to Conscience*, (Warner Bros., New York, NY: 2001), pp. 85-86.

[11] Knight, Walter B., *Knight's Treasury of Illustrations*, (Wm. B. Eerdmans Publishing Co., Grand Rapids, MI: 1963), p. 414.

[12] Johnson, p. 115.

[13] Tan, #6332.

[14] Ibid, #6334.

[15] Alexander, p. 10.

[16] Ibid, p. 37.

[17] Knight, p. 413.

[18] Fleet, James, *Hidden Power*, (Parker Publishing Co., West Nyack, NY: 1987), p. 41.

[19] Howell, p. 143.

[20] Carnegie, Dale, *How to Stop Worrying*, (Simon and Schuster, New York, NY: 1948), p. 96.

[21] Fleet, p. 1.

[22] Ibid, p. 5.

[23] Alexander, p. 58.

[24] Howell, p. 92.

[25] Tan, #4552.
[26] Howell, p. 66.
[27] Knight, p. 411.
[28] Ibid., p. 175.
[29] Knight, p. 175.
[30] Knight, p. 196.
[31] Alex., p. 256.
[32] Tan, #6301.
[33] Knight, p. 267.
[34] Knight, p. 272.
[35] Tan, #419.
[36] Knight, p. 18.
[37] Knight p. 2.
[38] Tan, #1891.
[39] Knight, p. 430.
[40] Howell, p. 28.
[41] Robinson, Ray, *Rockne of Notre Dame*, (Oxford University Press, New York, NY: 1999), p. 4.
[42] Knight, p. 115.
[43] Knight, p. 266.
[44] Felleman, Hazel, selected by, *Best Loved Poems of the American People*, (Garden City Books, Garden City, NY: 1936), p. 102.
[45] Knight, p. 115.
[46] Ibid., p. 411.
[47] Ibid., p. 411.
[48] Walton, Sam, *Made in America*, (Doubleday, New York, NY: 1992), p. 246.
[49] Tan, #2824.
[50] Alexander, p. 121.
[51] Johnson, p. 62.
[52] Alexander, p. 309.
[53] Knight, p. 30.

Books Written by JOY HANEY

At the Master's Feet
Behold the Nazarite Women
Blessing of the Prison, The
Breaking the Alabaster Box (cloth)
Call to Holiness, The
Call to Holiness (Spanish)
Carpenter, The (out of print)
Clean Out the Ashes (audio)
Diamonds for Dusty Roads, Vol. I (out of print)
Dreamers, The
Elite, The
Great Faith
Healing Power of Prayer, The
His Angels (cloth)
How to Forgive When It's Hard to Forget
How to Have a Wonderful Marriage
How to Have Radiant Health
How to Receive a Miracle
Kenneth F. Haney: A Man with a Vision
Living in the Miracle Level
Magical Gift of Kindness, The
May I Wash Thy Feet
Miracles Happen When Women Pray
Modern Day Abraham (out of print)
Nothing But the Best (out of print)
Phillip's Family
Pray the Word
Pressed Down but Looking Up
Privileged Woman, The
Put on Your War Coat and Fight!
Radiant Woman, The
Seven Parchments, The (out of print)
Those Bloomin' Kids

Victor, Not a Victim
What Do You Do When You Don't Feel Like Doing What You're Doing?
When God Doesn't Deliver on Time
When Mothers Touch Heaven (cloth)
Woman's Cry for Love, A

Women of the Spirit Series
Vol. I: Love, God's Way
Vol. II: Faith, Prayer and Spiritual Warfare
Vol. III: All About Trials
Vol. IV: Wisdom, Attitudes and Character
Vol. V: Women of Compasssion
Vol. VI: The Power of Praise
Vol. VII: JOY
Vol. VIII: FRUIT of the Spirit

The "When Ye" Series
When Ye Pray
When Ye Fast
When Ye Give
When Ye Fast (Spanish)